Praise for *The Kindness Workbook*

'A beautiful and accessible book to boost your wellbeing with KINDNESS by two of the leading compassion focused therapists working with young people'

— Professor Paul Gilbert OBE, founder of Compassion Focused Therapy and bestselling author of *The Compassionate Mind*

'*The Kindness Workbook* takes you on a journey of self-discovery and is packed with interactive exercises and creative interventions that will help you learn to be kinder to yourself'

— Emma Seppälä, PhD, Director of Stanford University's Center for Compassion and Altruism Research and Education and bestselling author of *The Happiness Track*

'This entertaining book is full of practices that young people can do to be kinder to themselves. As the authors show, self-kindness is key to happiness and wellbeing'

— Kristin Neff, PhD, Associate Professor at the University of Texas, Austin. Pioneer in the field of self-compassion and bestselling author

'A cornucopia of creative ideas for young people, parents, teachers, therapists and anyone who is interested in boosting wellbeing'

— Professor Sam Cartwright-Hatton, Professor of Clinical Child Psychology, University of Sussex

'Throughout your whole life, caring and kindness will lead you to greater emotional and psychological health. This excellent workbook will be your guide'

— Dennis Tirch, PhD, founder of The Center for Compassion Focused Therapy, New York City

'This beautiful and welcome book takes us through what it really means to integrate kindness into our 'selves', and is a must-read for, well . . . everyone'

— Dr Andrew Reeves, Associate Professor in the Counselling Professions and Mental Health

'A warmly written book, useful for clinicians and people reading on their own. It's fab!'

— Dr Lucy Maddox, Consultant Clinical Psychologist and bestselling author of *Blueprint*

Dr Elaine Beaumont is an accredited psychotherapist specialising in cognitive behavioural therapy (CBT) and compassion focused therapy (CFT). Elaine works with a range of charities and organisations and with young people who have experienced trauma. She is a lecturer in counselling and psychotherapy at the University of Salford, where her research explores the impact that cultivating compassion has on wellbeing. Elaine provides workshops for a variety of organisations, charities and the NHS, and her research has been presented worldwide.

www.beaumontpsychotherapy.co.uk

Dr Mary Welford is a consultant clinical psychologist who has held senior positions at the British Association for Behavioural and Cognitive Psychotherapies (BABCP) and Compassionate Mind Foundation. Mary currently works with a range of UK-based schools and heads up Care to Achieve, promoting the aims of educational settings via improvements to staff, student and parental wellbeing.

www.compassioninmind.co.uk

Also by Elaine Beaumont and Mary Welford

The Compassionate Mind Workbook by Chris Irons and Elaine Beaumont

The Compassionate Mind App by Chris Irons and Elaine Beaumont

Compassion Focused Therapy for Dummies by Mary Welford

The Power of Self-compassion by Mary Welford

The Compassionate Mind Approach to Building Self-confidence by Mary Welford

K ss
M ok

CREATIVE AND COMPASSIONATE WAYS
TO BOOST YOUR WELLBEING

Illustrations by Phoebe Munday

ROBINSON

ROBINSON

First published in Great Britain in 2020 by Robinson

3 5 7 9 10 8 6 4 2

Copyright © Elaine Beaumont and Mary Welford, 2020

The moral right of the authors has been asserted.

A CIP catalogue record for this book
is available from the British Library.

ISBN: 978-1-47214-327-3

Typeset in Palatino by Initial Typesetting Services, Edinburgh
Printed and bound in Great Britain by Bell and Bain Ltd, Glasgow

Papers used by Robinson are from well-managed forests and other responsible sources.

Robinson
An imprint of
Little, Brown Book Group
Carmelite House
50 Victoria Embankment
London EC4Y 0DZ

An Hachette UK Company
www.hachette.co.uk

www.littlebrown.co.uk

Contents

Acknowledgements

We would like to thank all of our clients (past and present) and all the young people we have worked with over the years. Working with you, witnessing your strength and courage, is a privilege and a pleasure. You have inspired us to write this book and remind us both every day that *kindness is key.*

Thank you to staff and students at the University of Salford who tried out many of the exercises in the book and gave valuable feedback about what worked and what didn't!

Many thanks to Cheryl Delisser, John Beaumont and Helen Millar for generously providing feedback on our earlier drafts.

Thanks to Andrew McAleer, Rebecca Sheppard and Sue Viccars at Little, Brown for your guidance and support.

Phoebe, thank you for using your creative skills and imagination to help bring the book to life.

Thank you to all the people who have supported and guided us over the years. There are too many to name but you know who you are – we are grateful to you all.

It's been **Eat, Sleep, Write, Repeat** for quite some time, so we definitely want to say thank you to friends and family who have supported, encouraged, fed and watered us.

A special thank you to Sue Massey for your encouragement, creative ideas, attention to detail and support.

Introduction

WELCOME TO *THE KINDNESS WORKBOOK*!

Growing up is a juggling act. Our bodies and hormones change, usually at the same time as important decisions about our future need to be made. We often put extra pressure on ourselves, compare ourselves unfavourably to others and worry excessively about what other people think. Add in exams, interviews, relationships, social media, peer pressure, celebrity culture and everyday stressors and it's no wonder our wellbeing can take a nosedive (we're exhausted just writing this!).

This is exactly why we recommend KINDNESS as a way of responding to ourselves and others.

So, if you feel life is a juggling act, you're not alone (although you're likely to feel as if you are).

What do we mean by kindness?

'Kindness is the language which the deaf can hear and the blind can see.'
– Mark Twain, author of *The Adventures of Huckleberry Finn*

If you look up the word 'kindness' you'll probably find something along the lines of: '*the quality or act of being helpful, caring, considerate, generous, gentle and thoughtful*'. So, kindness is:

- Caring for ourselves and other people

- Doing things that are helpful and improve the wellbeing of ourselves and others

- Being considerate of our own needs and the needs of other people

- Being gentle, patient and tolerant of ourselves and others

- It's common for us to show more kindness *to* others and receive more kindness *from* others, than show kindness to ourselves.

- Learning to be kind to ourselves, although difficult at times, can boost wellbeing.

The benefits of kindness

Think back to a time when someone was kind to you, maybe after a setback or disappointment. How did it make you feel? In that same situation, were you kind to yourself? Make some notes in the space below.

Imagine a friend had experienced the same setback or disappointment. What would you say to them?

Is there a difference between what you might say to someone else and what you would say to yourself? Do you fall into the trap of having one rule for other people and another for yourself?

You may have noticed that you tend to be more critical of yourself than you are of other people. Interesting, isn't it? We hope you'll come to discover that learning to be kinder to yourself will make a big difference to your wellbeing. If you're kind to *yourself* (and therefore less critical) you're likely to:

- Feel more confident

- Do the things you've always wanted to do

- Be more assertive and stick up for what you believe in

- Challenge yourself

- Learn from your mistakes (rather than avoid making them at all costs)

- Take part in activities, even if you're afraid

- Experience less anxiety, low mood and/or frustration

Of course, being kind to yourself is easier said than done, so as you progress through *The Kindness Workbook*, you'll learn different techniques that are 'kindness in action'. The skills you'll learn will help boost your wellbeing and reduce self-criticism and self-doubt. It's about learning to be kinder to yourself and being your own best friend rather than your own worst enemy.

Let's have a look at the popular legend of the Two Wolves, as it's a nice example that demonstrates the battles we all have going on inside us.

The Two Wolves

One evening a grandfather was teaching his young grandchildren about the internal battles each one of us faces. *'There are two wolves fighting inside each of us,'* he said. *'One wolf is vengeful, angry, resentful, self-pitying and scared . . . the other wolf is compassionate, joyful, generous, kind, faithful, hopeful and caring . . .'* The children thought about this for a moment or so and one asked: *'Which wolf wins, Grandfather?'* The grandfather smiled a knowing smile and replied, *'The one you feed.'*

While you progress through this workbook, you'll learn to feed the compassionate, joyful, generous, kind and hopeful you!

More about this book

The Kindness Workbook will take you on a journey of discovery. By the end you'll:

- Understand yourself and others more

- Appreciate what makes you tick, so you can put your efforts into being the best version of YOU (rather than trying to be someone you're not and exhausting yourself in the process!)

- Recognise the benefits of attention, mindfulness and imagery, and learn simple and effective ideas about how and when to use them

- Develop ways to boost your physical health, feelings, thoughts and behaviours and, in doing so, improve your wellbeing so that you can get more out of life

- Set a direction of travel for the future so that you can continue your kindness journey as you move forward

> *'Create a life that feels good on the inside instead of a life that looks good from the outside.'*
>
> – Unknown

Let's take a closer look at some of the therapies, practices and approaches that have influenced *The Kindness Workbook*.

Approaches That Have Influenced *The Kindness Workbook*

Acceptance and Commitment Therapy (ACT)

ACT focuses on learning to accept the struggles we face in life instead of avoiding them. ACT also helps us to take action by figuring out what we value in life.

Cognitive Behavioural Therapy (CBT)

CBT focuses on how *thoughts* (I'm not good enough, no one likes me), *physiology* (our body, its functions, physical sensations), *feelings* (afraid, sad, angry) and *behaviours* (run away, avoid fears, lash out, use recreational drugs or alcohol) influence each other. Making changes in these areas can boost wellbeing.

Compassion Focused Therapy (CFT)

CFT recognises that we all face struggles in life and focuses on helping us develop compassion for ourselves and others. CFT involves being sensitive to our own and other people's distress and uses a variety of creative approaches, including letter writing, imagery and method acting, to help us cultivate compassion and enhance wellbeing.

Counselling

Counselling uses compassion, curiosity, creativity, non-judgement, acceptance, congruence and empathy to help us nurture our true potential, understand ourselves and find solutions to problems.

Expressive Therapy

Creative strategies such as music, art, vision boards, writing and imagery have been found to accelerate learning while also helping us to express feelings, problem-solve, develop confidence and take helpful risks that embody change.

Mindfulness

Mindfulness is a way of being that focuses on training our minds to be in the present moment (*the gift of now – the present*) without judgement.

Narrative Therapy

Our lives can be greatly influenced by the stories we (or others) create about us. Narrative therapy encourages us to reflect on our lives and experiences, recognises the skills, knowledge and values we have, and aims to help us explore what we think is possible for ourselves in the future.

Positive Psychology

Rather than focusing on difficulties or problems, this branch of psychology emphasises the positive aspects of our experiences that are key to happiness and wellbeing. Bringing attention to positive experiences that make our lives worth living, and finding ways to increase them, can give our wellbeing a boost.

Whether you're reading this on your own or with a partner, parent, friend, counsellor or psychotherapist, the exercises, illustrations and worksheets will help you progress through the book.

Book structure

You're currently reading our Introduction, which allows us to say hello and set the scene for your kindness journey. You'll then find fourteen chapters, organised into three parts. We end the book with a Finale, which we hope will help focus your mind and energy on moving forward, equipped with skills you've acquired and a positive direction of travel.

Part 1 The Start of Your Kindness Journey

Part 1 outlines what is meant by 'wellbeing' and provides you with a memory aid (or mnemonic – harder to say and spell!), that spells the word **K.I.N.D.N.E.S.S.**, which focuses on some of the helpful things you're already doing that boost your wellbeing and gives you additional ideas to try. It suggests a framework for *understanding yourself* (AND others) with kindness at the core. It will also help you to explore the *values* you hold, so you can use them as a compass to guide you throughout life.

Part 2 Building Blocks for Everyday Life

Part 2 focuses on the skills of *attention*, *mindfulness* and *imagery*. On their own and collectively, these practices can really enhance wellbeing. These skills will also provide the building blocks to help you progress through the book.

Part 3 The Fabulous Four – Physiology, Feelings, Thoughts and Behaviour

Part 3 focuses on *physiology* (or 'body' for short), *feelings*, *thoughts* and *behaviour*. You'll discover they are all important and distinct aspects of your life, yet they all influence and interact with each other. Understanding the effects the 'fabulous four' have on you will enable you to make changes that will boost your wellbeing.

The book finishes with a 'Finale' and a farewell. Hopefully the last few pages will help you reflect on your kindness journey and help you to make a commitment for the future. At the end of the book we've created a Resource Bank so you'll have extra copies of the worksheets we've used.

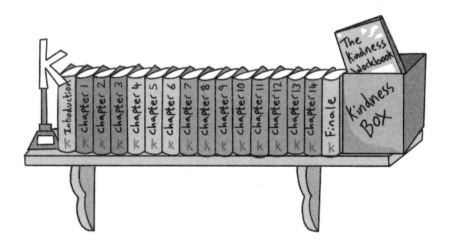

Throughout the book, we encourage you to engage with a range of creative exercises. For example, you'll focus on how to use music and lyric writing to help when you experience difficult feelings. You'll put yourself into the shoes of your favourite detective or Superhero in order to examine the evidence for and against thoughts. You'll also connect with your Kindness Crusader, Coach or Cheerleader, who will motivate and remind you to be kind to yourself, especially when you're facing challenges. Vision boards and other creative activities, which focus on what you would like your future to look like, and a variety of case examples will bring the ideas in the book to life.

You may find that there are sections you simply want to skim-read. For example, you might already be very aware of your feelings, their names and how they affect you. If this is the case just lightly engage with the material because – you never know – you might pick up a helpful hint, a slightly different piece of information or practice to help you. It's also important to note you're 'invited' to try the exercises outlined in this book. But if paying attention to your breathing or focusing on your body is tricky (for example, due to health issues), it's totally fine not to do it. As an alternative you might choose to think hypothetically about the exercise in question or get someone else to work with you.

Icons

The Kindness Workbook uses a number of icons to help signpost different sections. You may have noticed a couple already. Let's have a closer look so that you know what to watch out for:

This icon denotes *Top Tips* to help you gain more insight and understanding.

Taking time to *Reflect* can supercharge learning and, ultimately, accelerate improvements in wellbeing. Reflecting with kindness rather than criticism is of key importance. So, when you see this icon get your self-reflection ready and use the space provided to make some notes.

Sometimes it's helpful to briefly consider (rather than fully engage with) a scenario. When you see the *Imagine* icon, you'll be invited to think about something, for a short time.

Examples help bring ideas to life. They aim to give a better understanding of a situation someone is struggling with and help illustrate an important idea, point or issue. The examples we have used in *The Kindness Workbook* are fictional, although they do represent real experiences.

This icon identifies points that might be particularly worth remembering. As you work your way through *The Kindness Workbook* it can be helpful to recap different sections, especially those we've highlighted by use of the *Remember* icon.

Are you someone who likes to know a bit about science, and the research on which something is based? If so, the *Science* icon will direct you towards information that might be of particular interest to you.

If you're going to make changes to your wellbeing, it's a good idea to experiment! Exercises such as moving your attention and practising mindfulness will be preceded by the *Experiment* icon. It's helpful to engage with them with openness and curiosity. We hope some of them will become an important part of your everyday life.

The more we use a new skill the easier it becomes to master it, so this icon will encourage you to *Practise*.

Finally, you'll be introduced to the idea of creating your very own *Kindness Box*. Whenever you see this icon you'll be encouraged to add something to it. Additions may relate to the chapter itself or simply something that's come to mind while reading it.

As you work through *The Kindness Workbook* you'll become familiar with the icons, but until then, it might help to tag the page so you can refer back to it when clarification is needed.

How to use this book

The Kindness Workbook is full of information and has a variety of exercises for you to try out and incorporate into your day-to-day life. As such, try *not* to treat it as a sprint or even a marathon! Go at your own pace. You may need additional materials for some of the creative exercises. You'll be able to download information and interactive exercises from the website https://overcoming.co.uk/715/resources-to-download.

Your Kindness Box

Throughout *The Kindness Workbook* we focus on how you can create, and add to, your very own 'Kindness Box'. This could be used to store photos of places, pets or people, lyrics, playlists, vision boards, mind maps, quotes, beads, soothing and calming objects, letters, fluffy

teddy bears, shiny stones, pamper products and anything else that will help boost your wellbeing. Your Kindness Box will help you during the course of this kindness journey and in years to come, especially when things are not going to plan.

What will you need?

You might choose to buy, make, reclaim or repurpose (from another function) your box. You might decorate or paint it as a starting point, or as your kindness journey continues through the workbook. You may want something that's small enough to go under your bed or sit on a shelf, or you may decide to use a drawer or a big box that you can keep in a special place. If you're not a *stuff* person, you may decide to use your phone and/or tablet to store music, photos or inspirational quotes instead.

The important thing is to create something that's of benefit to *YOU*, so it can be whatever you want it to be!

Take your time

Learning to ride a bike, swim or learn a new language takes time, and of course patience. Be kind to yourself along the way – if you have a bad day and things don't go to plan, that's OK. Tomorrow is a new day fresh with its own possibilities, adventures or even mistakes!

'When failure is not an option, we can forget about creativity, learning and innovation.'

– Brené Brown

The Kindness Workbook focuses on learning strategies that will help you navigate your way through life. Small steps can make a big difference and each one is a victory, so remember to give yourself a pat on the back as you work through the book. Some people find it helps to make a plan or set a certain amount of time aside to work through each chapter. Other people like a team approach and may find it helpful to work through the book with a friend or family member.

Recognising what you're juggling

As discussed at the start of this Introduction, it's likely you're juggling a lot of different things at the moment, so it might help to start by noting them down on the juggling balls below.

Adding words to one, or more than one, of the balls is a good way of recognising the things you're balancing – even if you're not as 'in control' of them as you would want to be. We can't promise to solve all of life's difficulties, and we definitely don't have a magic wand, but we hope the ideas in *The Kindness Workbook* will help you navigate the ups and downs of life and ultimately boost your wellbeing.

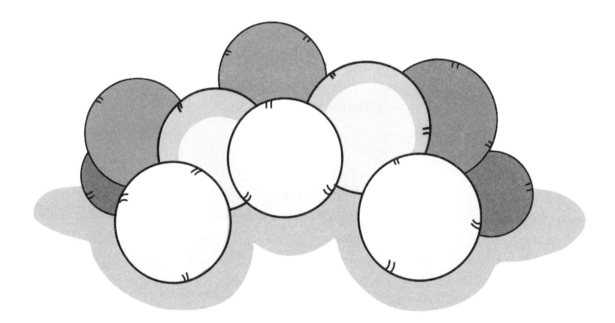

A little bit about us

We're Elaine and Mary, and we grew up in the days of avocado bathroom suites and swirly carpets (although they might make a comeback!), when people queued in the rain to make a call from a phone box. We'd travel with our families (often arguing) in the back of a car with no seatbelts! We didn't have computers or laptops, and one of the first computer games we can remember playing was PONG (check it out on YouTube). We rode bikes, read comics and books, and played football and tennis outside with friends.

So, how can you relate to us? Well, adolescence brought challenges for us. We both lacked confidence and sometimes felt inadequate. We both coped in different ways, sometimes positive and sometimes negative. When it comes to stuff like this, it really doesn't matter what year you were born. Even though your experiences will be different from ours, you may still feel the same insecurities.

So, why are we telling you this? Well, because we wish we could turn the clock back and tell our younger selves some of the amazing things we've learnt in our personal and work lives. If we had known then what we know now it may have prevented the worry, undermining thoughts and self-doubt. Obviously, we can't turn back time. We're not Doctor Who, and to be honest knowing what we know now means that we wouldn't want to change our history! But we do want to pass on some of the things we've learnt that may help you, so maybe . . . just maybe . . . you won't criticise or be unkind to yourself the way we sometimes did when we were growing up.

Being kinder to yourself

The Kindness Workbook is about learning to be kind to yourself, being your own best friend rather than your own worst enemy. We hope that you enjoy the many creative exercises we've included.

The book is 'a modern guide for everyone' (instead of a purely problem-focused self-help book) and will help equip you with the tools needed to navigate through the difficulties of life. With that in mind, the earlier you have access to the ideas the better but, by the same token, there is no better time to start than now – whatever your age.

So welcome – and let's begin!

THE START OF YOUR KINDNESS JOURNEY

Part 1 lays the foundation for your kindness journey. Chapters 1, 2 and 3:

* Considers what we mean by the term 'wellbeing'

* Gives you a framework for understanding yourself (AND others)

* Explores the values you hold, so that you can use them as a compass to guide you through life

In this section, Connor and Robin will come along for the ride, bringing the exercises to life.

1 What is wellbeing?

There are millions of answers to this question but, in a nutshell, wellbeing simply means 'being well'! Our wellbeing is made up of two vital ingredients: our **physical health** (which we tend to know and talk about quite a lot) and our **mental health** (how we think and feel about ourselves, other people and the world around us). So, if you're in pain *or* feeling down, it's likely your wellbeing will take a nosedive. And if you're in pain *AND* feeling down, then life might be very difficult indeed.

The Kindness Workbook will help you work on both these areas of your life because they are both really important.

In this chapter, you're going to:

- Explore the relationship between mental health, physical health and wellbeing
- Look at strategies to enhance wellbeing
- Consider what helps and hinders wellbeing
- Develop wellbeing skills
- Think about what to add to your Kindness Box

Appreciating different aspects of wellbeing

Recognising the importance of physical health has resulted in an array of activities and materials aimed at enhancing it. They include an abundance of magazines and books, TV programmes, gyms and (love it or hate it) even physical education (PE) on the national curriculum. In a bookshop the physical health section is usually where people are happy to hang out.

In contrast, mental health has historically been associated with negativity, stigma and taboo. If someone is interested in improving their mental health, there is often the assumption that there's something wrong with them, they must be weak in some way or that 'they're having problems'. This means many people fail to access information that would be helpful to them and, more worryingly, if people do have problems they are more likely to suffer in silence. This often results in more isolation, self-criticism, self-doubt and other difficulties.

Thankfully, the tide is turning and there's an increasing number of celebrities, bloggers and sports personalities promoting ways to improve mental health, in the same way as they share ideas about diet and fitness. Strategies are now shared, not only as a means to assist wellbeing, but also as a way to enhance performance, from 'getting into the zone' within sport (Tom Daley practises mindfulness to clear his mind and body of anxiety before he dives headfirst from a 10m platform!), to evoking an alter ego to play a character on stage (Beyoncé channels her alter ego Sasha Fierce when she's performing).

There's also a growing number of people bravely talking about times when their mental health has been put under great strain. Prince William and Prince Harry have openly discussed the impact losing their mum had on them, while Cara Delevingne, George Ezra, Sam Smith, Dwayne (The Rock) Johnson, Taylor Swift, Freddie Flintoff and many others have helped challenge some of the stereotypes associated with mental health. This supports the notion that we all struggle at times and this isn't something to feel shameful about – we wouldn't feel ashamed if we had a broken leg, so why should we feel ashamed if our mental health is in need of a boost?

So, whether you're interested in improving your mental health and wellbeing from a perspective of *'things are OK at the moment'* or reading this because you're struggling with anxiety, low mood, problems with food, or any other issue, you're in the right place – and you're not on your own.

Let's take a look at some of the things that influence our physical and mental health.

What affects our physical health?

The body we have, the activities we engage in, the food we eat and the quality and quantity of our sleep all affect our physical health. While some people sleep like logs and find exercise a breeze, others find it all a bit trickier. While some people have to endure growing pains, diabetes, asthma, headaches or restricted diets, others seem to sail through life without any such difficulties.

What affects *your physical health?*

You could write about things that have happened in the past or things that are happening at the moment. Some of these may have a positive impact on your physical health, while others may have a negative impact on you.

_____

_____

_____

What affects our mental health?

Our life experiences (the impact events have on us), our genetics (the body we have, aspects of our personality and temperament), and the religion and culture we're born into (the norms affecting us) all have an impact on our mental health. Sometimes the impact is big, sometimes it's small, sometimes it's positive and other times it's negative.

What affects your mental health?

You could write about things that have happened in the past or things that are happening at the moment. Some of these may have a positive impact on your mental health, while others may have a negative impact on you.

_____

_____

_____

We'll look at this in more detail in Chapter 2, but for the time being simply recognise some of the factors that influence your wellbeing.

- If you wanted to improve your physical health, build muscle and become healthier, you would exercise and alter your diet. In a similar way, if you wanted to improve your mental health, you would learn to be kinder to yourself and engage in exercises that boost your wellbeing.

- If you're struggling with how you feel right now, that's OK – we all struggle at times. The key to improving wellbeing is knowing exactly what can help.

Physical and mental health in combination

Although we often think about mental and physical health separately, it's helpful to recognise how much they influence each other. For example, if we're physically injured we're more likely to worry and feel down. Equally, if we're sad we might not have the same level of energy as we would when excited and happy, which might mean we exercise less. This could impact negatively on our mood because we may not be as physically strong as we would like.

Can you remember a time when your physical health wasn't so good? Maybe you were worried about your health, or were unable to see friends because you were unwell. How did this affect your mental health?

REFLECT

_____

_____

_____

Can you remember a time when your mental health wasn't so good? Maybe you were less physically active, struggled to sleep or regularly experienced a racing heart. How did this affect your physical health?

_____

_____

_____

Thankfully, it works in the opposite direction too! When we're feeling physically well, our mental health gets a boost; and if we're feeling mentally strong, our body can often feel stronger too. So, _both_ our mental and physical health have an individual _AND_ combined impact on our wellbeing.

The role of kindness

We've discovered that kindness is '*the quality or act of being helpful, caring, considerate, generous, gentle and thoughtful*', so it's great to cultivate and practise it, especially when growing up and when we're juggling *SO* many things.

We've created the mnemonic K.I.N.D.N.E.S.S. as a prompt to help you focus on some of the key (kindness) ingredients that will help you build and maintain your wellbeing. They relate to aspects of your physical and mental health. We've given an outline and a few examples for each letter of the mnemonic. Once you've read through the examples, consider the things you're already doing and think about areas you may wish to expand or introduce. Further chapters will hone in on insights, ideas and activities in much more detail, but the memory aid is a great place to start.

Making a start on your kindness ingredients

The worksheet on pages 24–25 poses a range of questions to prompt you around each of the eight K.I.N.D.N.E.S.S. ingredients. It's likely you're doing a range of activities under each heading already, so start by making notes about these, because they may be things you want to maintain or increase. Then spend some time thinking about what would be helpful to try. Make notes in the space provided in the worksheet.

TOP TIPS

- Consider what your friends and family do that makes them feel good, or maybe get their input on ideas that might be of benefit to you.

My Kindness Worksheet

K.I.N.D.N.E.S.S. Ingredients	Examples	What I do already and what I'd like to try
Keep learning It's common to feel a sense of wonder and/or achievement when you've learnt something new, be it mastering a new song or learning about the natural world. What would you like to learn about or do?	*Reading a book, following a nature trail, doing a crossword or puzzle, learning to play a musical instrument, visiting a museum or animal sanctuary.*	
Interact Interacting, connecting and communicating with friends and family can boost wellbeing. How could you interact and communicate more?	*Joining a team, group or a band, going out or visiting family or friends, arranging a party or playing a game.*	
Notice It's important to notice and acknowledge how you feel. Do you notice when your mood takes a nosedive and when it gets a boost?	*Asking for help when you need it (or noticing when someone you care about needs help), talking to friends, family, work colleagues or a therapist. Remember it's 'OK not to be OK'.*	
Decide Making decisions that have your wellbeing at heart can help you live a fulfilling life (instead of a life that's driven by fear or avoidance). What decisions can you make that are good for your wellbeing?	*Making plans for your future, having a hobby, enrolling on a course, setting yourself a challenge, facing fears.*	

Nurture Being kind to yourself. If you're having a bad day, think about what will help you feel better. How do you look after yourself and how might you build on that? Does it help to have 'time out' on your own when things are difficult, or does it help if you're around animals or nature?

Asking yourself 'How can I show myself kindness today?' Painting a picture, being in nature, listening to music, watching a comedy, talking to somebody or writing about how you feel. Remember if things don't go your way, be kind to yourself.

Exercise Being active increases the release of feel-good hormones and exercise can help you connect with other people. What physical activities do you like to do and what activities might you want to try?

Going for a walk, trying a fitness app, working out, trying a new exercise class with a friend, taking your dog or a neighbour's dog out for a walk.

Self-care Looking after your physical and mental health can give your wellbeing a boost. What could you improve? What helps you relax or have fun? What can you do to pamper or treat yourself?

Having healthy eating and sleeping habits, having your hair cut, going to a spa, buying yourself some flowers, going to the beach, acknowledging achievements.

Support others A kind word or gesture can brighten up somebody else's day and make you feel good. How could you support others?

Volunteering to help others, being involved with a charity, giving somebody a compliment, being kind to somebody by sending them a supportive text message, card or note.

Now it's time to experiment. Maybe it's just a matter of trying the different things you've written down. Alternatively, you may want to ask someone you trust and like spending time with to help or work with you. You may find you need to problem-solve around potential barriers or break activities down into smaller, more manageable chunks. What's important is your direction of travel, so consider experimenting in any way that's right for you.

Having engaged in a new activity it's important to recognise how you feel. Would it help to repeat the activity, practise the activity or turn your attention to something else? Consider putting emojis, ticks or smiley faces on your worksheet to indicate the things you've done and how they've gone so you can track your progress. It's also helpful to write some notes about the changes you've made and about any plans you may have as you move forward. Is there anything you would like to continue to do or introduce in the future?

_____

_____

_____

Small changes can make a big difference.

- Don't set yourself up to fail – that's not good for anyone. Pick things that appear to be manageable.

- If you were unable to achieve your goal or it didn't go to plan, try not to criticise yourself. Instead, consider what you would say to a friend in the same situation. Try saying the exact same thing to yourself and, importantly, in the tone of voice you would say it to a friend. Then, as you would in a game of chess, have a strategy in place and plan your next move.

- If you find something useful, why not do it again tomorrow, and the next day, and the next day . . .?

My Kindness Box

At the start of the book, we introduced the idea of creating a Kindness Box. This is somewhere you can put things that help you focus on kindness and is something that reminds you that you can boost your wellbeing. You'll see throughout the book we continue to refer to the Kindness Box. You may prefer to call it something else or use

something other than a box. You may prefer to call it a wellness bag, first aid box, kit bag, setback plan or even a kindness shelf. The key is to have somewhere to store things that act as reminders to you to be kind to yourself.

Remember this is your box (or virtual box), so it can be whatever you want it to be. As we touched on in the Introduction, your Kindness Box could include things such as pamper products, photographs or pictures, poems or lyrics to music that you like, a list of TV programmes that uplift you or make you laugh, a soothing or calming object, a fluffy teddy bear, a shiny stone or a smell that comforts you. To start with, you may just want to include *The Kindness Workbook*!

When you think about what you would like to put into your Kindness Box it may be helpful to ask yourself these questions:

- What helps me when I'm not feeling at my best – does writing, listening to music, talking to friends, drawing, painting and/or physical exercise help? Would it help me if I have a playlist, art supplies or photographs of things I like in my box?

- Who helps – who makes me feel better about myself or cheers me up? Could I put a photograph of that person (or animal) in my box?

- Where helps – do I like going to the cinema, sitting in the garden, watching football and/or going to the park? Could I put photographs of places I like in my box? Would they help me feel better when I'm having a bad day?

In the subsequent chapters, we'll return to the idea of the Kindness Box, but for now here's a recap of what we've covered in this chapter.

Summary

In this chapter, you have:

❖ Considered what wellbeing means

❖ Explored the relationship between mental and physical health

❖ Looked at how you can boost wellbeing

❖ Examined some of the key 'Kindness Ingredients' that help improve wellbeing

❖ Started to think about the things you would like to include in your Kindness Box that will remind you to be kinder to yourself

Additional notes

What will help me be kinder to myself?

What can I add to my Kindness Box?

2 Understanding yourself and others

You'll probably agree that we're born into a compli-cated world, with a complex mind and body that we don't choose. We don't come with a 'how to' instruction manual telling us how to navigate life's challenges; and even if we did it would be impossible to digest due to the infinite possibilities and pitfalls our biology and life experiences can create.

It's helpful to realise that we're not perfect and that many of us feel *'the odd one out'* or *'the imposter'* with amazing regularity. To add insult to injury, we have a body that simply works against us at times: we have to contend with blushing, body odour, spots and nerves, making us even more anxious exactly when we want to appear cool, calm and collected. These are just some of the things we sometimes have to deal with.

Some of our coping strategies are really helpful, while others can cause us more problems than they solve. We can find ourselves in a spiral of self-blame, shame and self-doubt. To improve our wellbeing, it's helpful to understand (as much as we can) ourselves. We can then turn our attention to understanding others.

In this chapter, you're going to:

- Think about your biology and experiences and how they influence the person you are

- Examine some of your worries, fears and concerns

- Notice the coping strategies you use and explore the benefits and drawbacks of these strategies

- Create a mind map

- Bring your observations together before considering how we're all more similar than different

- Think about what to add to your Kindness Box

- Focusing and reflecting on the material in this chapter may be an emotional process. As such, it can be helpful to work through it in stages, taking breaks as and when you need to. You may prefer to work through other chapters first and come back to this one when you're ready to look at the things that influence the person you are. Alternatively, recruit the help of someone you trust who has your best interests at heart.

Understanding ourselves

Learning to understand ourselves requires patience and kindness, so be kind to yourself as you engage in the following six steps.

1   Considering your biology and experiences

2   Identifying worries, fears and concerns

3   Noticing your coping strategies

4   Exploring the benefits and drawbacks of your coping strategies

5   Creating a mind map to explore helpful ways of coping

6   Putting it all together

Throughout the chapter, we'll focus on Connor's story to help you navigate the step-by-step process.

Connor struggled with self-confidence. He had a lisp, which he was embarrassed about, and often put himself down. He avoided making eye contact with people he didn't know that well because he thought they would judge him.

Step 1 Considering your biology and experiences

From conception, our *biology* predisposes us to certain characteristics. Our genes influence our temperament, emotional and intellectual intelligence, physical health, body shape and height. This is often referred to as our **nature**.

Such attributes are not set in stone because our *experiences* also play a role. For example, we may have the potential to reach a certain height (biology), but if we don't have access to a healthy diet (experiences), this potential might not be realised. Our innate temperament (biology) might be introverted and shy, but if we have a large, sociable family, we may have learnt to successfully navigate such gatherings (experience) and may behave like an extrovert for limited periods of time. Such influences are often referred to as our **nurture**. Let's have a look at some examples of biology and experiences that may apply to you.

- *Biology*-wise, you may be naturally sporty, have freckles or blush easily. Maybe you matured early or late, are prone to spots or were much taller or smaller than your peers at particular points growing up.

- With respect to your *experiences*, maybe you went to a busy school or were home schooled. Maybe you had loyal friends or were bullied. Maybe teachers and/or your parents made certain subjects enjoyable. Perhaps you learnt multiple languages from an early age.

In this next section, spend some time thinking about how your biology and experiences in life have affected and influenced you.

Biology

How have your physical attributes and learning style influenced the person you are today? What attributes might you have inherited from your biological parents?

_____

_____

_____

Connor wrote:

> I'm male, I have a lisp, I'm not very tall, I'm sporty like my parents and I have freckles.

Early life experiences and family relationships

How have relationships with your parents and siblings impacted on you? Have religious, cultural and societal factors influenced you? For example, there may have been messages regarding what feelings it's OK to show, how you should behave, what you should look like and whom you should be attracted to.

_____

_____

_____

Connor wrote:

> My sister teased me because of my lisp so we didn't really get on. My grandparents were 'old school'; I liked them but they had one rule for girls and a different one for boys. Girls shouldn't get angry and boys shouldn't cry. My parents were quite easy going and were very loving.

Education and work

Think about school, home, college, work and social groups. How have they, or the people there, influenced you? Did (do) you enjoy or avoid certain subjects and activities? Do you have any career aspirations?

_____

_____

_____

Connor wrote:

I enjoyed school. I liked to learn but was shy in class. I didn't like the focus to be on me because I struggled with my lisp. I was good at sports and played in a football team but avoided drama when I could! I have a part-time job coaching young children. I like what I do and want to eventually finish my coaching qualification and get a full-time job coaching.

Peer and romantic relationships

How have relationships with your peers impacted on you? Did (do) you have positive or difficult relationships at school? How have romantic relationships affected you (think about the people you found attractive, dated or broke up with)?

_____

_____

_____

Connor wrote:

> I was concerned and embarrassed about my lisp when I was at school and I still am. We moved around a lot which was difficult because I always felt I was starting again. I've always been shy around girls and I've always worried that I'm being judged because of my lisp.

Reviewing your life in this way may help you realise that many of the things you might feel self-critical about are not your fault and are not of your making. If there are things that you consider were under your control and were of your choosing, attempt to meet this with kindness instead of criticism – no one's perfect, and we can all benefit from being kinder to ourselves.

Step 2 Identifying worries, fears and concerns

Our mind can play host to an infinite number of worries, fears and concerns that can feel overwhelming. Spending time exploring these can make them a little less scary and more manageable.

One way to 'break them down' is to notice those that are triggered by our *external world* (environment) and those that originate in our *internal world* (within us). Here are some examples to help illustrate this.

External world	Internal world
External worries, fears and concerns may include worrying about what people think or feel about us. We may worry or fear rejection or we may be concerned that people may make fun of, criticise or withdraw support from us. We may fear or worry about people harming us. An approaching storm, strange noises, foul smells, hospital appointments, relationships, exams, interviews or news stories might also trigger worries, fears and concerns.	Internal worries, fears and concerns may include being concerned that we're not good enough, that we're a failure, that we'll be lonely and disconnected from other people. We can even worry about worry! We may worry about our health or certain bodily functions such as eating, going to the toilet or being sick.

Let's have a look at Connor's worries, fears and concerns. When you're ready, make some notes about any you have, thinking about them in terms of your external and internal world.

Worries, Fears and Concerns Worksheet

Connor's external Worries, fears and concerns	My external worries, fears and concerns
People will judge me (because of my lisp) other people won't want to be my friend – they'll look down on me	
Connor's internal worries, fears or concerns	**My internal worries, fears or concerns**
I'm concerned I'll never be able to manage this anxiety I worry that I'll never be able to make meaningful connections I worry that I'll always struggle in social situations	

REFLECT

Having written your worries, fears and concerns on the worksheet, consider which one you would like to work on. Do any jump out at you? Maybe there's one that has a significant impact on your wellbeing.

The worry, fear or concern I'm going to focus on today:

Connor decided he wanted to focus on his fear of being judged by other people. He felt that his fear of being judged was central to many of the difficulties he had.

Once you've decided on the worry, fear or concern you want to work on, take a look at Steps 3, 4 and 5.

Step 3 Noticing your coping strategies

We're all trying to get by, in a complicated world with a complex mind and body. To do so, we engage in protective behaviours designed to help us. Some are conscious, such as double checking we've locked the front door, while others are unconscious, such as breathing rapidly. Collectively we refer to them as **coping strategies**.

We all tend to use a range of coping strategies *Before, During* and *After* situations. They can be incredibly helpful; after all, how many of us pack an umbrella just in case it rains!? However, some strategies can also be unhelpful. For example, being passive or criticising ourselves for the way we look or how we perform in an exam is likely to undermine our confidence *and* make us feel bad. Take a look at some helpful and unhelpful strategies to see if there are any that you identify with and place a tick next to any that apply to you.

Before difficult situations do you:

- Talk yourself out of doing something because you're worried about what other people might think

- Overprepare

- Engage in rituals (this might involve saying, thinking or doing something over and over)

- Practise mindfulness or relaxation exercises

- Plan to avoid certain people (which might be very helpful!) or certain conversations

- Engage in 'practice runs' before visiting somewhere new or call a venue in advance to check there are toilets, parking and other facilities

During difficult situations do you:

- Monitor what you're saying and/or keep discussions short

- Try to please others

- Focus on your breathing

- Speak fast, wring your hands and/or focus on the facial expression of others

- Reassure yourself you're taking a step in the right direction *or* undermine your efforts

- Touch a particular item of jewellery or a talisman

- Use mantras

After difficult situations do you:

- Ask for feedback or reassurance

- Discount positives

- Replay events over and over

- Zone out with food, vomit, self-harm or take recreational drugs

- Criticise yourself

SCIENCE

Although some of your body's coping strategies for dealing with threatening situations are meant to be helpful, they can actually be really problematic. For example, an increased breathing rate gets us ready for fight or flight, which is incredibly important if there's a lion after you! But 'over-breathing' can make us feel dizzy and result in us getting hot, going red and/or shaking, which isn't so good if we're giving a presentation! Of course, these are unconscious coping strategies; people don't generally choose to overbreathe, for example, but it's useful to notice them because we can then do something about them.

The next exercise focuses on identifying the coping strategies you used in a situation when your worry, fear or concern (from Step 2) was triggered. Let's take a look at Connor's worksheet as an example. Connor focused on some training he had attended at work.

Connor's Coping Strategies Worksheet

My worry, fear or concern	Situation that last triggered a worry, fear or concern	Coping Strategy Before	Coping Strategy During	Coping Strategy After
People will judge me because of my lisp	Attending training that involved having to speak in front of a group of people	Got there early so I knew I could get a seat that wasn't in the eye line of the workshop leader I made sure Beth was going because I knew if she was, I'd be okay doing a role-play with her	Avoided eye contact with the workshop leader Spoke quietly hoping people didn't hear me Consciously slowed my breathing down to help me to relax	I discounted positives I didn't talk it through when I got home I gave myself a talking to because I'm such an idiot — getting worried about something so lame

Have a look at the worksheet and start by writing, in the first column, the worry, fear or concern you've decided to focus on. In the second column make note of a situation that triggered the worry, fear or concern. In columns three, four and five, consider what your coping strategies were *Before, During* and *After* the situation. What did you do or not do?

My Coping Strategies Worksheet

My worry, fear or concern	Situation that last triggered a worry, fear or concern	Coping Strategy Before	Coping Strategy During	Coping Strategy After

It can be helpful to repeat this process whenever you notice you're worried, afraid or concerned.

Because we're *SOOO* complex there's a huge array of coping strategies you might employ, and with each advancement in technology year on year there's even more to choose from! Your great-great-grandparents didn't have the means to take a reassuring photo of an unlit candle to prove the house wasn't going to burn down, and they definitely didn't have hair straighteners to double and triple check to make sure they were unplugged before going to bed!

Step 4 Exploring the benefits and drawbacks of your coping strategies

We've discovered that we're all the product of our biology and life experiences (Step 1), much of which wasn't our choosing. We've learnt that we all have worries, fears and concerns (Step 2), plus an array of coping strategies (Step 3) to help us navigate through life. It's now time to consider the benefits and drawbacks of your coping strategies. It's likely some will be helpful in the short, medium and long term. However, others may cause unintentional problems. For example, avoiding eye contact may be helpful for Connor in the short term, because he may not be asked a question and then have to speak in front of people. However, in the long term it doesn't give him the opportunity to speak when he knows the answer to a question, so he doesn't get the chance to give his confidence a boost. Here are a few examples to help you think about the benefits and drawbacks of coping strategies:

- You might manage your exam worries in the short term by going out, watching a box set or even tidying up instead of revising, but overuse of these strategies might mean you're less likely to get the grades you're capable of.

- Saying yes to every social event, for fear of missing out, might mean you're always in the thick of it and having fun, but in the long run it might mean you're exhausted and fatigued, unable to do other things due to lack of energy or lack of cash!

- Concerned about losing your friend on a trip to the city might mean you check your phone is fully charged before setting off – and theirs too. All very sensible, but what if you end up constantly checking the amount of charge you have and end up being distracted? What if your friend gets annoyed because you also keep asking them to check theirs too?

- Having a couple of drinks on your own before a night out may calm your nerves, but could mean you're not in sync with the people you're meeting. In the long term, this might not be so good for your health either.

Step 4 involves considering the benefits and drawbacks of your coping strategies. Before you complete your own worksheet, have a look at Connor's.

Connor's Benefits and Drawbacks Worksheet

Benefits of my coping Strategies	Drawbacks of my coping Strategies
Avoiding eye contact means I'm less likely to be asked questions	I don't get to meet other people as much as I'd really like to
I feel less anxious in the short term because I stay in my comfort zone	I don't give myself the opportunity to share what I know
It's less stressful doing a role-play with someone like Beth who I know and get on with	I get annoyed with myself
	It stops my confidence growing and makes my anxiety worse in the long run

What are the benefits and drawbacks associated with the coping strategies you use? If it helps, look back at the coping strategies you listed in the previous step.

My Benefits and Drawbacks Worksheet

Benefits of my coping Strategies	Drawbacks of my coping Strategies

It's important to recognise the attempts you've made to address your worries, fears and concerns. *Be kind to yourself* even if you can see that some of the things you're doing are unhelpful in the short or long term. You've been doing your best, but maybe now it's time to give yourself a helping hand so that you can make some changes.

Step 5 Creating a mind map to remind yourself of helpful ways of coping

Having considered one of your worries, fears or concerns, the coping strategies you use, and their potential benefits and drawbacks, it's time to consider what might be useful going forward. A helpful way of doing this is by creating a mind map that identifies:

- Supportive and useful coping strategies that will be helpful to continue to use

- Strategies to use with caution

- New helpful strategies that might be worth trying

Have a look at the stages involved and at Connor's answers before you complete your own mind map. There is a blank one for you to complete at the end of the four stages listed below. The examples of new coping strategies on page 48 will help if you hit a roadblock.

The stages involved in the development of your mind map are:

1   On your mind map write the specific worry, fear or concern you've been focusing on, placing it in the circle, in the middle of the page. Connor wrote: '*People judging me*'.

2 Think about the coping strategies you already use, that would be *helpful* to continue. On your mind map, mark these entries by using the word 'current' along a line connecting it to the circle. These entries recognise and remind you of the things that are working already. Connor wrote: '*Remind myself a lisp bears no relation to the person I am*' and '*Use techniques to help me slow down and relax*'.

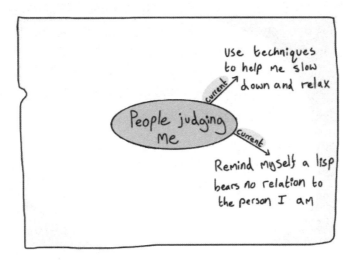

3 Now turn your attention to coping strategies that help you in the short term but come with the potential for long-term *drawbacks*. Mark these entries with the word 'caution' along a line connecting it to the circle. Connor wrote: '*Avoid eye contact*'. Connor found this helpful in the short term, because it meant he didn't tend to get asked questions he didn't know the answer to, but realised this was a strategy to use with caution because it didn't help him build his confidence in the long term or share the answers he knew!

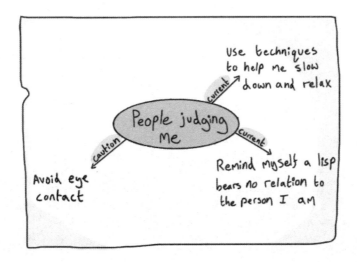

4 Finally, consider *new helpful* ways of coping (that will help you in the long term) or even new ways of thriving, and add these to your mind map. Mark these entries with the word 'new' along the line connecting them to the circle. Connor wrote a personal mantra to help reassure himself when he felt anxious: *'I'm doing the best I can right now'*. He then thought about practising building his confidence with people with whom he felt comfortable, and wrote *'Beth would be good to practise with'*. Connor wanted to remind himself that some people like him and don't judge him, so he wrote *'Remind myself that some people do like me because they ask me out'*. He also decided that he needed to remind himself not to treat himself unfairly, so he wrote *'Be kinder to myself'*. Finally, he wrote *'Speak to my boss'*, as he knew she was approachable and thought this might result in helpful discussions about new strategies he could use at work.

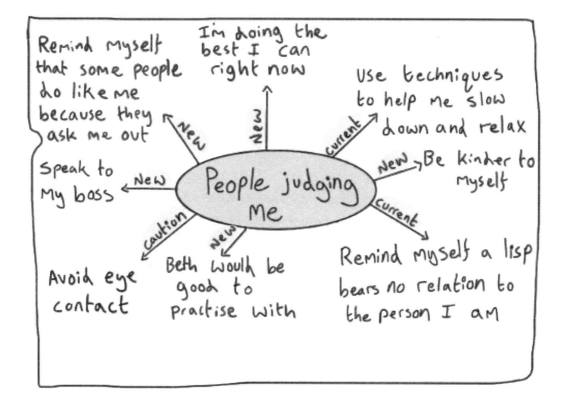

- If you want to get more creative, use a variety of colours to show the different categories of coping strategies. For new coping strategies, you could use the colour green to remind you of new shoots of growth, new life and new beginnings – with which you need to be gentle and encouraging!

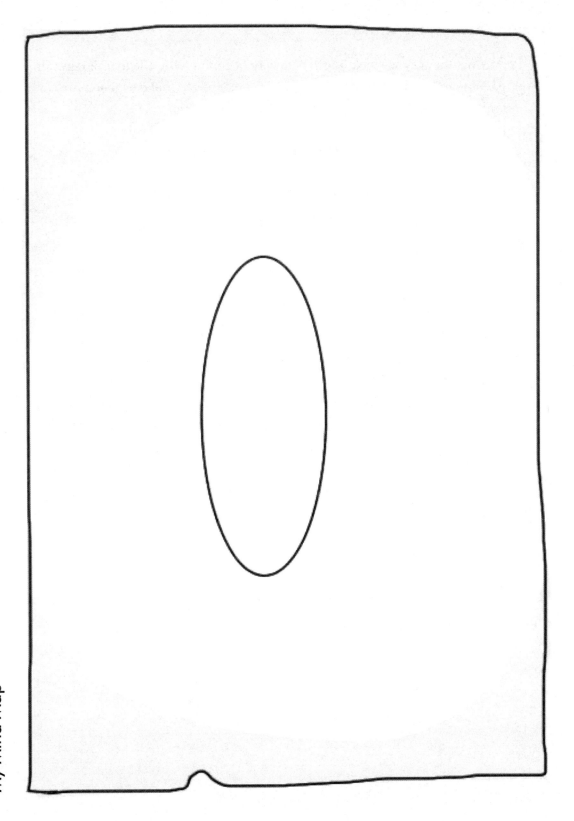

My Mind Map

Exploring new coping strategies

- 'Perfecting' the way we look might be a way of coping with the fear of rejection or judgement. In the short term, this coping strategy might make us feel more confident and may be helpful in certain situations. However, it might actually make us more anxious in the long term, feeding the idea that others will reject or judge us if we didn't put so much effort in. The *green shoots* of a new coping strategy might involve warmly reassuring ourselves that looks aren't everything, and speaking to ourselves in the same way we would speak to a friend struggling with the same thing.

- Concerns about our future, and our role in it, might result in us using an array of avoidance strategies. For example, we may absorb ourselves in gaming, box sets, eating, drinking, excessive exercise or even self-harm. In the short term this might distract us from sad or anxious feelings, but in the long term this may lead to addiction or we might miss out on new opportunities and feel even worse. As such, it can help to consider which coping strategies are helpful or unhelpful and which to use in moderation or with caution. The green shoots of new coping strategies might involve being a bit more open with a family member or friend. It might mean being a bit more open with yourself, too. Writing about how you feel with kindness and care and thinking about what you would say if you were speaking to a friend who might be struggling in the same way can also be helpful.

Having completed Steps 3, 4 and 5, for one specific worry, fear or concern, consider if it would be helpful to focus on any of the others that you identified in Step 2. You might do this straight away or at a later date. Before you know it, you might have a number of really helpful mind maps.

Life continues to throw up new experiences, challenges and insights (even when we're old and wrinkly), so it can help to return to the exercises in this chapter again and again.

Step 6 Putting it all together

It can be helpful to bring together the steps covered in this chapter so that you can see your answers in one place. Have a look at the worksheet provided, and the entries Connor began to make, before creating your own.

Connor's Understanding Myself Worksheet

STEP 1

My biology
I have a lisp
I am male
I'm not very tall
I'm sporty
I have freckles

My experiences
Teased by my sister
My grandparents were 'old school'
Loving parents
Didn't talk much
Moved schools

STEP 2

Worries, fears and concerns

External
People will judge me (because of my lisp)

Other people won't want to be my friend – they'll look down on me

Internal
I'm concerned I'll never be able to manage this anxiety
I'm worried I'll never be able to make meaningful connections
I worry I'll always struggle in social situations

STEP 3

Current coping strategies

Before: Arrived early, went with someone I'm comfortable with and reminded myself that a lisp bears no relation to the person I am

During: Avoided eye contact, spoke quietly and consciously slowed my breathing down

After: Discounted positives, didn't talk it through and gave myself a talking to

STEP 4

Benefits of current strategies
Avoiding eye contact means I'm less likely to be asked questions
I feel less anxious in the short term because I stay in my comfort zone

Drawbacks of current strategies
I don't get to meet other people as much as I'd like
I don't give myself the opportunity to share what I know
I get annoyed with myself

STEP 5

New strategies that will be helpful in the long term
• Remind myself I'm doing the best I can right now
• Practise with Beth and speak to my boss
• Remind myself that some people do like me because they ask me out
• Be kinder to myself

Understanding Myself Worksheet

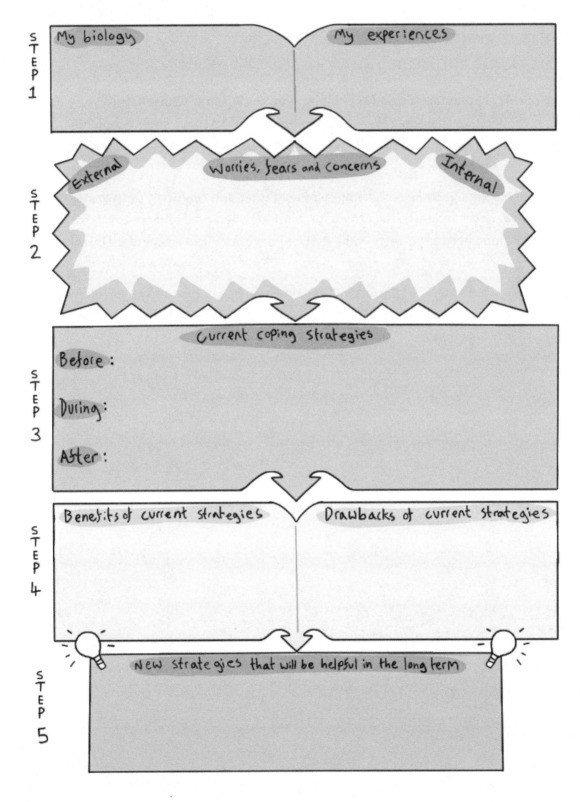

STEP 1

My biology   My experiences

STEP 2

External   Worries, fears and concerns   Internal

STEP 3

Current coping strategies

Before:

During:

After:

STEP 4

Benefits of current strategies   Drawbacks of current strategies

STEP 5

New strategies that will be helpful in the long term

'We have all come on different ships, but we're in the same boat now.'

– Martin Luther King

Pause and consider how similar we all are

Most of this chapter has focused on helping you understand yourself, but we're missing a trick if we don't use the same knowledge to help us understand other people too. After all, when we realise how similar we all are, it can help us feel less critical and judgemental and more connected to others.

Although our coping strategies change across cultures and centuries, our worries, fears and concerns vary very little. The majority of us want to be accepted and approved of. Most of us have a profound need to be 'seen', validated and have our efforts recognised by other people.

Let's start by considering someone you like and know quite well. What might have shaped the person they are today? Think about their biology and life experiences.

REFLECT

_____

_____

_____

Are you aware of any worries, fears and concerns they have?

_____

_____

_____

Now think about how they cope. How helpful are the coping strategies they use?

_____

_____

_____

Of course, if we like someone, this can be a relatively easy exercise. It can also give us a few ideas about potential changes we might make when we interact with them. The exercise can be tricky when we focus on someone with whom we have difficulty; however, this can be an equally – if not more – powerful exercise and is one to consider trying.

Understanding someone's behaviour doesn't mean we have to excuse it. However, it can help us see another person's actions (or inactions) as less personal. Think back to your first year at high school. While many kids kept their heads down and found themselves desperately trying to fit in and develop a sense of belonging, others might have spent

their energy attempting to claim their place as 'alpha' or 'top dog'. It can be helpful to see these behaviours as different coping strategies, with benefits and drawbacks to individuals *and* those around them.

It can also be helpful to remember that we all have similar worries, fears and concerns, we all have mental health just as we have physical health and we're all born into cultures, families and countries that we don't choose.

We're now at the end of this chapter. Well done on working through the steps. Let's take a look at potential additions to your Kindness Box.

My Kindness Box

What would you like to add to your Kindness Box? Could you include something that reminds you that we're all more similar than different, that we're all the product of our biology and our life experiences, most of which is not under our control and not of our choosing? You might choose to add photos reminding you that experiences have shaped the person you are or something to signify the role evolution has played. How about adding your mind map or an image of it? Finally, would it be helpful to take photographs on your phone of the images or worksheets you've created? You'll then be able to look at them whenever you choose and use them as a portable reminder of what's in your Kindness Box and your journey so far.

Summary

In this chapter, you have:

❖ Considered the impact of your biology and life experiences

❖ Recognised worries, fears and concerns

❖ Examined and explored the benefits and drawbacks of your coping strategies

❖ Created a mind map focusing on helpful coping strategies

❖ Brought all your observations together by completing the Understanding Myself Worksheet

❖ Paused and considered how similar we all are

❖ Considered additions to your Kindness Box

Additional notes

What will help me be kinder to myself?

What can I add to my Kindness Box?

3 Identifying your values

You probably know what music you enjoy listening to, what you like watching or playing, how you like your hair and what food you love (and hate!), but are you aware of the values you hold? Despite the fact that our values guide us, give our lives purpose and meaning and impact on our wellbeing, most of us don't know what they are. Values differ, person to person, and can change over our lifetime, depending upon our experiences. When our values are put 'into action', our wellbeing gets a boost, but when our values are compromised (by ourselves or other people), this can cause us problems.

In this chapter, you're going to:

- Explore your values

- Think about ways you can put your values into action

- Consider what might get in the way

- Create an image of a tree, which focuses your attention on your values

- Think about what to add to your Kindness Box

Your values and you

In Chapter 2 we discovered how our biology and life experiences influence who we are. Much of who we are is not of our choosing. For example, we have no control over the country we're born in, the family we're born into, or the colour of our skin or hair. Thankfully, as we become more self-aware and independent, we can begin to consciously nurture ourselves and our wellbeing. We can also begin to make helpful (if sometimes anxiety-provoking) choices: for example, whether to break a habit of a lifetime and volunteer for public speaking, or go for that rather radical hair style!

Building on your work so far, it's now time to consider your values so that you can use them as a lifelong compass. Let's start by seeing if you can identify some of your values. We'll share Robin's story throughout this chapter, so you can see her examples.

Identifying your values

There are literally hundreds of different values we might hold. In the book *The Happiness Trap,* Russ Harris provides a description of some of the most common ones. We have been given permission to share some of these with you, so you can use them as prompts during this next exercise.

Start by reading through the list of values and put a tick in the box next to those you initially identify with. If there's a value that's important to you that isn't on the list make a note of it in the space provided. It's probably best to whittle them down to the five or six values that give your life most meaning.

Let's take a look at the list of values.

Values	My Top 6
Adventure To be adventurous; to actively seek, create, or explore novel or stimulating experiences	
Authenticity To be authentic, genuine, real and be true to myself	
Caring To be caring towards myself, others and the environment	
Challenge To keep challenging myself to grow, learn and improve	
Compassion To be sensitive to distress (be it other people's or my own) and motivated to prevent and/or alleviate it	
Connection To engage fully in whatever I am doing, and be fully present with others	
Contribution To contribute, help, assist or make a positive difference to myself or others	
Cooperation To be cooperative and collaborative with others	
Courage To be courageous or brave; to persist in the face of fear, threat or difficulty	
Creativity To be creative or innovative	

Equality To treat others as equal to myself, and vice versa

Excitement To seek, create and engage in activities that are exciting, stimulating or thrilling

Fairness To be fair to myself or others

Fitness To maintain or improve my fitness; to look after my physical and mental health and wellbeing

Freedom To live freely; to choose how I live and behave, or help others do likewise

Friendliness To be friendly, companionable or agreeable towards others

Fun To be fun-loving; to seek, create and engage in fun-filled activities

Generosity To be generous, sharing and giving, to myself or others

Honesty To be honest, truthful and sincere with myself and others

Humour To see and appreciate the humorous side of life

Industry To be industrious, hard-working and dedicated

Independence To be self-supportive, and choose my own way of doing things

Intimacy To open up, reveal and share myself (emotionally and/or physically) in my close personal relationships

Justice To uphold justice and fairness

Kindness To be kind, compassionate, considerate, nurturing or caring towards myself or others

Love To act lovingly or affectionately towards myself or others

Open-mindedness To think things through, see things from others' points of view and weigh evidence fairly

Persistence To continue resolutely, despite problems or difficulties

Respect To be respectful towards myself or others; to be polite, considerate and show positive regard

Safety To secure, protect or ensure the safety of myself or others

Self-care To look after my health and wellbeing, and get my needs met

Self-development To keep growing, advancing or improving knowledge, skills, character or life experience

Sexuality To explore or express my sexuality

Spirituality To connect with things bigger than myself

Trust To be trustworthy; to be loyal, faithful, sincere and reliable

My values are:

1. _____

2. _____

3. _____

4. _____

5. _____

6. _____

How easy or difficult was it to whittle your values down to five or six? Maybe you're a bit of a rebel and settled on four or seven! Did any of the values you chose surprise you? Did you think of a value that wasn't listed? What do you think about the values you identified with?

_____

_____

_____

- Values are about what gives your life meaning rather than what you want to get or achieve.

- It can be tempting to pick specific values because you believe you should, but this might not be what makes your life meaningful.

- Just as a tree adapts and flexes to its environment, values can also change over time.

Let's take a look at Robin's story.

Robin decided on connection, fun, fitness, self-development, creativity and challenge. She reflected that over the last few months she'd been spending lots of time working. As such, Robin hadn't had time to do the activities that were consistent with her values and realised that this might account for why she wasn't feeling so great.

Values 'in action'

When we engage in activities consistent with our values, we say our values are 'in action'. So, if you value *open-mindedness*, you might go along to a debate, carefully listening and weighing up both sides. Open-mindedness would not just be 'in action' during the debate. It would have guided your decision to attend the debate and it would be present afterwards, if you mull over the opinions you had heard. Before you take a look at when each of your values are (or have been) 'in action', take a look at Robin's list for a few ideas.

Robin placed each of her values in the first column. She then took some time to consider good examples of her values 'in action'. Some activities appeared more than once; for instance, family night (on a Tuesday) made two appearances, while Sunny (her dog) made multiple!

Robin's Values In Action Worksheet

Value	Examples of Values 'in action'
Connection	Spending time with good friends, family night, Skyping Sarah, lying with Sunny on the sofa, visiting the sea
Fun	Swimming, parties, holidays, playing with Sunny, family night, going to a comedy club, going to the theme park
Self-development	Reading this book, learning Spanish
Fitness	Walking and running with Sunny, swimming, dance classes, park run
Creativity	Drawing, painting, playing music, creating dance routines
Challenge	Duke of Edinburgh Award, learning to surf, rowing for charity, training Sunny

REFLECT

Write down each of your values and make a note of times when they are 'in action'.

My Values In Action Worksheet

Value	Examples of Values 'in action'

Understanding the impact values have on wellbeing

If we live with our values central to our lives, our wellbeing can flourish. However, if our values are disregarded (by ourselves or others) or have no outlet our wellbeing can suffer. Let's take a closer look at the impact your values have on you.

REFLECT

Read through the examples of your values 'in action' from the previous exercise. Each value will have a different impact on you. For example, going swimming with friends will be a different experience from bird watching, even though they might both be examples of your values 'in action' and you might love both. How would you collectively summarise the impact your values 'in action' have on your wellbeing?

Robin wrote:

Life has so much more meaning when my values are 'in action'. It's helpful to keep them all in mind and have them as key ingredients for my week.

Consider your values and think about times when it's been difficult for your values to be 'in action'. What impact did that have on you? How did that impact on your wellbeing?

Robin wrote:

Extra work is good financially but too many shifts have a negative impact on my mood. I tend to feel a sense of dread on a Sunday when I'm preparing for a long working week. I miss out on exercise and social events...and creativity goes out the window! All in all too much work isn't great for my wellbeing.

Understanding blocks and making adjustments to our lives

Understanding the link between our wellbeing and values is an important step towards being kinder to ourselves – when we understand why we're stressed, down, angry or anxious we're less likely to beat ourselves up. In addition, understanding what might block our values 'in action' can give us ideas about new options to try. Although some blocks are relatively easy to overcome, others are trickier to manage. Take a look at the chart to get an idea of how values can be blocked.

Blocks that get in the way of living life in accordance with our values

Sometimes our wellbeing takes a nosedive because our values are inhibited due to circumstances outside our control. Here are a few examples:

Independence might be compromised if we live at home with our parents or have to return to live there.

Work environments where *humour* is looked down on might mean we have to be more serious than we want to be.

Valuing *cooperation* might mean we enjoy teamwork but means that we could potentially find it difficult to be happy in an organisation that's highly competitive.

Health difficulties such as pain might stop us being so *persistent* with an exercise programme.

Sleep problems may affect our capacity to be *industrious*.

Overwhelming anxiety and worry might get in the way of *adventure* and *intimacy*.

Strong urges, addictions and compulsions might prevent us from *connecting* with ourselves and others.

If blocks are getting in the way of you living your life in accordance with your values, have a look at the next exercise and complete the worksheet on page 63.

Make a note of each of your values on the worksheet and then consider if there are any blocks getting in the way. For example, *creativity* might seem blocked by approaching exams, or an injury four weeks before a charity half marathon, might block the value of *challenge*. Consider what other options might be open to you that will bring your value to life. For example, assisting your revision with the creation of eye-catching mind maps might be an outlet for your creativity, while raising money for a friend, still in the race, might be a great way of harnessing your love for a challenge.

My Values, Blocks and Options Worksheet

Value	Block/s	Option/s

Placing our values (visually) at the centre of our lives

Pictures, posters and vision boards are just some of the ways we can use our creativity to express our feelings, remind us of what's important and to inspire and motivate us. They can create a snapshot of our lives and a vision for our future. When we generate images and graphics that focus on recognising, appreciating and understanding ourselves, we can experience an enhanced sense of identity – an identity that's unique to us.

The next exercise focuses on creating a tree of life – an image that places your values where they belong, central to your life. Your tree will also include aspects of your unique biology and life experiences and examples of your values 'in action'.

It can be helpful to think of your biology (nature) as the *roots* of a tree, your experience (nurture) as the *nutrients* that both feed and then become part of the tree itself and to think of your values as the *stem* or *trunk* (stem in our youth, trunk for us oldies!). Values can create structure and a direction of travel. Just as the stem or trunk connects and supports the *crown* (branches, leaves and everything else), your values connect you to what's important, supporting your growth.

You'll find an outline of a tree on page 67 for you to use for this next exercise and an example of the tree Robin created on the following page. Alternatively, you might prefer to create your own illustration, so that you have more space to add photos, mementos (such as gig tickets), pieces of material (reminding you of a person or activity) and cards. Unsurprisingly, given her value of creativity, Robin used a foam board, instead of paper, and pinned photos, cards and mementos onto her tree. Whether or not creativity is one of your values it might help to see how imaginative you can be with the exercise, so try to bring your tree to life!

Robin's Tree of Life

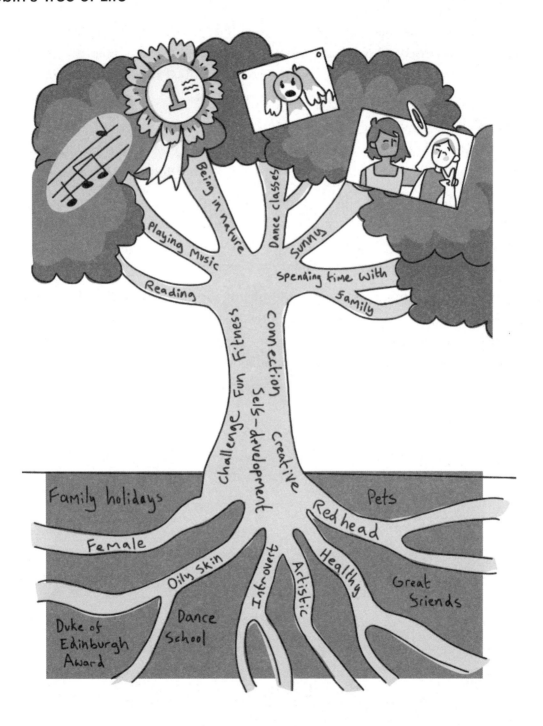

Create your own tree in four steps

1.   It might help to refer back to Chapter 2 to remind yourself of the key aspects of your biology and experiences. Add words to the roots of your tree that relate to your biology and words into the nutritious soil that represent your life experiences. You may wish to use multiple colours to represent different aspects.

2.   Now add your values to the stem or trunk. It might help to write them vertically, to represent the fact that, just as the trunk connects a tree's roots to the crown, your values connect your biology and experiences with activities that give your life meaning.

3.   Now turn your attention to the branches. Add words and images to represent current times when your values are 'in action'. It might help to look back at the examples you generated earlier in the chapter. In addition, add words and images to signify more general activities that give your life meaning.

4.   Finally, is there anything else you would like to add that will remind you about your values? These will make up the foliage of the tree. Is there something that inspires and reminds you to put your values into action? Is there something you would love to do in the future? If there is, add some words or images to capture your ideas.

My Tree of Life

How does it feel to have created a tree that focuses on your life's journey and your values to date?

_____

_____

_____

Values provide us with a direction of travel and a way of living our lives. It's inevitable that we get caught up in seemingly important things and lose contact with what truly matters to us. But when we're aware that we're moving away from our values, we can make helpful adjustments to stop us going off track! Reviewing and reminding ourselves of our values on a regular basis can help us flourish.

In this chapter, you've focused on your values and reflected on what's important to you. So, before we end the chapter, it can be helpful to think about what you've found useful and what you would like to add to your Kindness Box that reminds you of the values you hold.

My Kindness Box

Would you like to add cards you've received that remind you of important connections, or some cash to buy yourself flowers if you're in need of a little self-care? Could you add something that reminds you of your spirituality or pictures that remind you of the beauty of the natural world? Would you like to add a few kind words to yourself in case you find your values have been compromised or not prioritised? Finally, how about adding a copy of your tree of life – or maybe it needs some sunlight, taking pride of place on a wall!

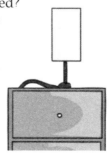

Summary

In this chapter, you have:

- ❖ Explored your values
- ❖ Considered how you can put your values 'into action'
- ❖ Identified blocks and new options for your values
- ❖ Placed your values, visually, at the centre of your life
- ❖ Considered additions to your Kindness Box

Additional notes

What will help me be kinder to myself?

What can I add to my Kindness Box?

PART 2

BUILDING BLOCKS FOR EVERYDAY LIFE

The chapters in Part 2 provide really important skills to improve wellbeing. They will also equip you with additional key building blocks that you will be able to use as you work through the rest of the book. Exercises will help slow down your busy mind and soothe away your worries. You'll also generate a virtual place where you can feel at ease, peaceful and calm. Amazing, eh?! The skills you'll acquire centre on:

- Attention

- Mindfulness

- Imagery

Throughout this section Mason, Alex, Carter and Malia will come along for the ride to help bring the exercises to life!

4 Using your attention as a spotlight

'Look on the bright side', 'Focus on the positive' and 'Don't dwell on the negative' might be some of the well-meaning advice you've been given at times, or even said to yourself! You may have thought 'That's easier said than done', but we can actually learn to 'move our mind' away from the negatives to more neutral or even positive stuff.

In this chapter, we're going to discover the power of attention and develop an increased awareness of its impact on us. We'll then explore how we can improve wellbeing by moving and redirecting our attention towards things that are helpful. These great skills also provide an excellent foundation for learning about mindfulness and imagery, which we'll explore later on in our Kindness Journey.

In this chapter, you're going to:

- Experience the power of attention

- Move your attention to different parts of your body, to memories and sounds

- Consider what it would be helpful to move your attention to

- Use prompts to remind you to refocus your attention

- Think about what to add to your Kindness Box

Moving your attention

Attention is like a spotlight. We can use it to bring things into sharp focus, while leaving others in the shadows. Knowing what's helpful to shine our attention on, and practising doing so, can have a positive impact on our wellbeing.

Have a go at the exercises to discover what happens when you move your attention. This will be the starting point of training your attention, in a way that's beneficial to you.

Moving your attention to your hands and feet

Sit comfortably and engage with each step of the exercise for about 30 seconds or so. You may wish to close your eyes. Perhaps try doing the exercise once with your eyes open and then with your eyes shut and notice if the lack of visual stimulus sharpens your attention.

1.   Bring your attention to the sensations in your left foot. Maybe focus on your toes, the sole of your foot, and the contact your foot has with the floor or your shoe.

2.   Repeat this, but now bring your attention to your right foot.

3.   Bring your attention to the fingertips of your right hand. Explore the sensations in your fingertips.

4.   Rub your fingertips against your thumb and experience the sensations associated with this movement.

5.   Repeat Steps 3 and 4 with your left hand.

Gently bring the exercise to a close and widen your awareness to the chair that's supporting you and the room that you're in. If your eyes have been closed, open them: lift your gaze. Take some calming breaths and maybe have a stretch before you write about what you noticed.

What did you notice when you moved your attention to your hands and feet?

_____

_____

_____

Mason experienced heightened sensations in each area of his body as he switched his attention. Alex noticed (as she put certain areas of her body into the spotlight) that other bodily sensations were less 'present'. Carter noticed tingling in his fingertips as his thumb rubbed against them and Malia noticed that switching her attention was relatively easy and quite relaxing.

Interesting, isn't it? We can consciously move our attention and, in doing so, experience different sensations in the part of our body that we're focusing on. Let's have a go at another exercise and explore how moving our attention to different memories impacts on our body, thoughts and feelings.

Moving your attention using memory

Bring to mind a time you found yourself really laughing. You may have been with family or a friend, maybe watching a film or TV programme. Re-familiarise yourself with the memory for 30 seconds or so.

What do you notice? How did bringing your attention to a happy memory influence your body, thoughts and feelings?

_____

_____

_____

Mason thought about a time when he was playing 'fetch' with his dogs Rosie and Ralph. He noticed that the fun memory made him feel happy and light.

Now move your attention away from the memory and focus on your breathing. Experience a sense of slowing down. Alternatively, you may prefer to focus your attention on sounds around you for a few seconds.

Bring your attention to a situation you've found difficult recently, nothing too emotional but something you feel OK to revisit for a short time. Maybe a situation that made you slightly anxious (for example, having to do a presentation), angry (having a disagreement with a friend) or sad (feeling disappointed when a friend didn't text you back). Re-familiarise yourself with the memory for 30 seconds or so.

What do you notice? How did bringing your attention to a difficult memory influence your body, thoughts and feelings?

_____

_____

_____

Alex felt a hint of sadness as she remembered her last day at school . . . she remembered thinking at the time 'I hope my school friends stay in touch with me.'

Now move your attention away from the memory and focus on your breathing. Experience a sense of slowing down. Alternatively, you may prefer to focus your attention on sounds around you for a few seconds.

Finally, bring your attention to something you recently enjoyed. Maybe time spent on your own or time spent with friends or family. Re-familiarise yourself with the memory for 30 seconds or so.

What do you notice? How did bringing your attention to an enjoyable memory influence your body, thoughts and feelings?

_____

_____

_____

Carter thought about a Christmas party he'd been to and smiled as he remembered showing off some moves on the dance floor. He remembered that he'd had great fun and his body felt energised at the time.

By intentionally calling to mind different situations, you may have experienced different feelings and bodily sensations. You may have also noticed that these were associated with different facial expressions and thoughts too. For example, when you reconnected with a time you were laughing you may have noticed you smiled or started laughing just thinking about the memory. These exercises have important implications for our wellbeing because they demonstrate that we can move our attention to what's helpful to focus on, and that we can practise moving our attention away from areas of difficulty.

The last exercise in this section involves switching between different sounds. You'll need to listen to a piece of music performed on multiple instruments. You can do a similar exercise in a range of situations such as tuning into different sounds when you're out in nature or in your house. You don't always have to have music to listen to, but it's a great starting point.

Moving your attention to different sounds

Find a place, away from distractions, where you can be for 10 minutes or so. A place where you can just focus your attention on a piece of music. Some people listen to instrumental music because they get distracted by words. You could try listening to both and see what works for you (just not at the same time!).

Attending to music

1. When you're ready, sit in an upright but relaxed position and close your eyes or choose a focal point to look at, such as the base of a picture frame or a mark on the floor. Notice the sensations you feel as you breathe slowly in and out.

2. When you're ready, notice the rhythm of the music. If your attention wanders, don't judge or criticise it – just bring your attention back to the music.

3. Spend a minute or so focusing your attention on a specific instrument (perhaps the sound of the guitar or the beat of the drum).

4. Move your attention to the speed of the music and notice how loud or soft it is.

5. If your music has vocals, switch your attention and focus on the artist's tone of voice and then the lyrics.

6. As you listen to the music, notice how it makes you feel. Do you feel calm, relaxed, sad, inspired, re-energised or peaceful?

7. Now move your attention to your breathing and heart rate. After 60 seconds or so switch your attention to your body and notice any other physical sensations that you're experiencing.

Gently bring the exercise to a close and widen your awareness to the chair that's supporting you and the room that you're in. If your eyes have been closed, open them: lift your gaze. Take some calming breaths and maybe have a stretch before you write about what you noticed.

How did it feel listening to the music? What did you notice as you moved your attention to different parts of the music?

_____

_____

_____

Malia noticed that she was able to easily switch focus to the different instruments and that the music made her want to dance.

Attention grabbers!

It's a fact of life that our attention is grabbed by potential **DANGER**. So it's helpful when our attention gets grabbed by a car driving towards us erratically, the foul smell of curdled milk or the pain of broken skin. This survival mechanism was really important for our ancestors and can still be really important for us today.

Many studies show that we naturally and automatically pay attention to things we see as threatening rather than positive. When ninety-nine smiling faces were presented on a screen and only one frowning face, researchers found (by tracking eye movements) that people were quicker to spot the odd one out – the frowning face – than when the experiment was reversed. Interesting, isn't it – our mind naturally focuses on what it thinks is threatening and negative.

Our attention is also grabbed by change. For example, if you're used to your desk being a certain way, your attention will be grabbed when something has been left on it or (even worse) something is missing! Attention grabbers fall into two broad categories – internal and external. Physical sensations, mental images, thoughts and feelings come from within us, so we call these *internal attention grabbers*. In contrast, noises, smells, someone's facial expression and wild animals are external to us, so they are referred to as *external attention grabbers*.

As you've worked through the exercises in this chapter, your mind may have been caught by different attention grabbers. You'll have probably worked out that it's good to notice where your attention is and then decide if it's helpful to hold that focus. If it isn't, the key is to kindly and gently move your attention and focus on what is helpful. This takes practice – just like learning to ride a bike – and is central to the practice of **mindfulness**, which you'll explore and learn about in the next chapter.

- When we're feeling down or anxious, our mood consumes us. It seems everything reminds us of how difficult things are. To counteract this, it can help to move our attention via multiple senses. For example, putting on our favourite jumper, spraying our favourite fragrance, playing a piece of music (that assists our mood) and flicking through specific photos is likely to help us move our attention.

- Learning to be the master of our attention doesn't mean avoiding the difficult stuff, it just means not having difficult stuff at the forefront of our mind all the time.

Deciding what to shine your attention on

You have learnt that attention is like a spotlight and can be moved, and that what you focus on influences your bodily sensations, feelings and thoughts. Whether you're having a tricky time (and your mind has become a playground for upsetting and worrying thoughts), or you simply want to reconnect with a sense of wellbeing, it can be helpful to consider what it might be useful to focus on (e.g. playing music or doing an activity) and move your attention to that.

- Just as you wouldn't learn to swim in the deep end of a swimming pool, starting to train your attention in really stressful situations isn't advisable either. It's helpful to begin when you're relatively relaxed and things are going OK – rather than start at a time when there are lots of attention grabbers around.

Consider moving your attention to things that might enhance your wellbeing. Is there a happy memory you can think about? Could you focus your attention on things you're looking forward to? For example, thinking about your pet waiting for you at home might give you a warm glow – or could looking through your Kindness Box at memories and mementos boost your mood? Is there a piece of music you can listen and attend to, or a blog or poem you like reading that you could focus on? How about bringing your attention to a smell you like?

What can I move my attention to when my wellbeing needs a boost?

Mason planned to think about his dogs Rosie and Ralph, Alex decided to look at photos in her Kindness Box and Carter thought about his next family holiday, whereas Malia decided on a song that she liked to dance to.

Now consider what might prompt you (at regular intervals during the day) to move your attention to things that help boost your mood. Maybe a photo next to your bed will prompt you to bring your attention to happy memories just before sleep. A shiny pebble in your pocket might trigger you to simply experience its smooth surface, while a scented candle might remind you to bring your attention to the experience of slowing down and breathing in the scent. A note on your mirror, a plant on your windowsill or the use of a specific mug to drink from might be helpful prompts too. Finally, could you use technology to remind you to switch your attention? How about setting reminders on your device, or use an app that randomly sends them?

What prompts could you use to refocus your attention?

_____

_____

_____

Studies have shown that our attention is often grabbed by novelty, so how about changing your prompts from time to time? Changing the photo, moving a plant or listening to a new piece of music may help you switch your attention to something that's positive or helpful. Choosing to refocus your attention will not change the world, but it can interrupt your tendency to live your life on autopilot. As you strengthen this skill it will help you break cycles of worry and rumination and will give your mind the mini-break it may need.

My Kindness Box

In this chapter, you've looked at how you can move the spotlight of attention. So, before we end the chapter, spend some time reflecting on what you've found useful. Is there anything you would like to add to your Kindness Box to remind you about how you can refocus your attention? After giving it some thought, Malia decided to add a note with the phrase, '_What I focus on expands_', to her Kindness Box as a reminder for her to switch her attention to helpful things. How about adding a pebble, photo, bracelet, scent or your favourite poem? In the next chapter, we're going to build on the insights you've learnt here by focusing on mindfulness.

Summary

In this chapter, you have:

❖ Focused on how to move the spotlight of attention

❖ Moved your attention to different parts of your body, memories and sounds

❖ Learnt that attention can be grabbed by internal and external attention grabbers

❖ Considered using prompts to remind you that you can refocus and tame your attention

❖ Reflected on what you would like to add to your Kindness Box

Additional notes

What will help me be kinder to myself?

What can I add to my Kindness Box?

5 Practising mindfulness

You may have heard about mindfulness. Over recent years, there's been an increase in its use in schools, colleges and workplaces. This is largely due to the recognition that practising mindfulness can have a positive impact on wellbeing.

In a nutshell, mindfulness involves paying attention, on purpose, to the present moment and doing so non-judgementally. We might consciously bring our attention to our breathing, sounds, smells, the movement of trees or the sensations we feel as our feet touch the ground. Just as you moved your attention in the previous chapter, mindfulness involves doing something very similar. However, this time we attempt to maintain a focus and, when we notice our mind has jumped to something else, we simply acknowledge this has happened and then return it to what we were focusing on.

In this chapter, you're going to:

- Become mindful of the present moment without judgement

- Focus on mindful breathing and mindful listening

- Explore how you can introduce mindfulness into your everyday life by using exercises such as mindful eating and walking

- Think about what to add to your Kindness Box

Studies have shown that the introduction of mindfulness in schools and colleges has helped students feel calm and relaxed and, in some cases, has helped them get better results in tests!

- Mindfulness involves a sequence of intentionally *focusing*, then *noticing* when your mind has wandered (maybe to what you plan to do that evening, what you did yesterday or what you wish you hadn't done!), and then *refocusing* again.

- *Mind wandering* happens to us all. 'Catching yourself' is the whole point of the exercise. So, when you notice your mind has gone down a rabbit hole of irrelevant or unrelated stuff, give yourself a brief pat on the back for noticing and then steer it back into focus.

Mindfulness exercises

In this section we're going to focus on four exercises. Mindful breathing and mindful listening can help slow down our bodies and are great starting points, so we'll begin with those. Later we'll look at mindful eating and walking. You can download recordings of the exercises at https://overcoming.co.uk/715/resources-to-download.

Preparation for mindfulness exercises

Start the exercises by finding a place where you can sit without being disturbed – somewhere that's free from distractions. It's worth reading through each exercise first to familiarise yourself with the flow. It can help to sit on a chair in an upright position, with your feet on the floor (shoulder-width apart), and your head also in an upright position. If you're listening to the audio you can begin by gently closing your eyes; if you prefer to keep your eyes open, focus your attention on something in front of you, such as the base of a picture frame or a mark on the floor.

Mindful breathing

In this first exercise we're going to focus on mindful breathing because this is something we can do anywhere and at any time.

Mindful breathing

1. Having found somewhere to sit and settled your mind and body, gently focus on your breathing, becoming mindful of it. Just notice the sensations as you slowly breathe in and out.

2. It may help to find a point to concentrate on. For example, some people find it helpful to focus their attention on the area around the tip of their nose, noticing the sensation of air as it moves in and out. Others find it helpful to pick a point in the centre of the chest, noticing sensations as their chest expands on the in-breath, and contracts on the out-breath. You may prefer to focus on the rise and fall of your belly as you breathe in and out. There's no right or wrong way of doing this; the key is just to notice the experience of each breath.

3. If you feel your breath is a little shallow or ragged, don't worry. It's more important to just be aware of the process and sensation of breathing, and mindful of how it feels to have air entering and leaving your body.

4. If your mind wanders, gently, kindly and without judgement, bring it back to your breathing. Mindfulness is just learning to observe (with curiosity) how your mind is working at any one moment.

When you're ready to bring the exercise to a close, gently widen your awareness to the chair that's supporting you and the room that you're in. If your eyes have been closed, open them: lift your gaze. Take some calming breaths and maybe have a stretch before you write about what you noticed.

What did you notice?

_____

_____

_____

Mason noticed the exercise helped calm him down, Alex noticed she wanted to fall asleep, Carter was amazed that the air felt colder on his tongue on the in-breath and Malia noticed that she started thinking about lunch, but was able to refocus on the exercise.

Mastering any new skill requires practice and patience, so be kind to yourself as you engage in the steps! Don't criticise or judge yourself if your mind wanders.

Remember, the whole point of being mindful is 'catching yourself' when your mind has drifted and just gently refocusing your mind.

Mindful Listening

In this next exercise, we're going to focus on mindful listening by spending time focusing on the sounds we can hear around us.

Mindful listening

1. Once again find somewhere to sit and settle your mind and body by gently bringing your attention to your breathing. Notice the sensations as you breathe slowly in and slowly out.

2. When you're ready, become aware of the sounds around you.

3. Notice as they change, as they come and go.

4. When you notice your mind has wandered, maybe to what's for dinner, or where a specific sound is coming from, gently bring the focus of your mind back to noticing sounds, as they occur, in the present moment.

5. Notice your ability to mindfully focus on one particular sound. Be curious to the type of sound. Is it a loud or quiet sound? Focus on the pitch and tone of the sound and whether it is continuous or irregular.

6. Continue this practice for 5–10 minutes.

When you're ready to bring the exercise to a close, gently widen your awareness to the chair that's supporting you and the room that you're in. If your eyes have been closed, open them: lift your gaze. Take some calming breaths and maybe have a stretch before you write about what you noticed.

What did you notice?

_____

_____

_____

Malia noticed that she really paid attention to the different sounds. She was distracted at one point by a loud sound that startled her, but was able to mindfully refocus on the pitch and tone of sounds.

Mindful breathing and listening are good examples of how to develop the skill of knowing where your mind is at any one time. The more you notice that your mind has wandered, the more mindful you are!

Mindfulness every day

It's helpful to practise mindfulness every day. This doesn't always mean finding a quiet place to sit. It might involve being mindful when we make a sandwich, brush our teeth, go for a walk or play a game. Often we travel from A to B, eat, drink or wash without focusing on what we're doing in that present moment. It's also easy to get caught up in thinking loops. For example, worrying about something that's happened in the past or about something that's coming up in the future. This is normal, but means we're allowing our minds to play unhelpful patterns through us, which often results in us feeling anxious, sad or stressed. It also means that we're not focusing on what's happening in the 'here and now'.

'All we know for sure is what we have this very moment. Maybe this is why it's called "the present" – because it can be a gift to us!'
The Compassionate Mind Workbook (Chris Irons and Elaine Beaumont)

Mindfulness is helpful because we learn to focus our mind on the present moment ('the gift of now'), leaving less space for rumination, worry or self-doubt. In the next two exercises, we're going to have a go at mindful eating and mindful walking so you can explore this for yourself.

Mindful eating

It's so easy to get distracted when we're eating, isn't it? We can get sidetracked by an alert on our phone, the TV or worrying thoughts that loop around in our mind . . . It's only when we notice that our food is too cold or too hot or that it tastes funny that we're really in the present moment. Mindful eating helps us to focus on the here and now so that we don't miss out on the potentially pleasurable experience of eating!

For this exercise you'll need to first decide what you want to eat! It might be helpful to start with something small like a piece of fruit or piece of chocolate. Mindful eating involves being in the present moment, instead of everywhere but! You might focus on the texture, taste, colour, sound and smell of the food. Once again find a place where you will not be disturbed.

Mindful eating

1. When you've decided what you're going to eat, spend a few seconds looking at it and notice how your body responds.

2. Gently pick up the food and focus on its shape, size, texture and colour.

3. Smell the food – what do you notice?

4. Notice the temperature of the food – is it hot, warm or cold?

5. Now taste the food. What flavour do you notice?

6. What does it feel like in your mouth? Think about the texture.

7. How does it feel to move the food around in your mouth and then to chew it?

8. Spend some time noticing how it feels to swallow the food and how you feel when you've finished eating.

When you're ready, bring the exercise to a close and gently widen your awareness to the room. Take some calming breaths before you write about what you noticed.

What did you notice?

_____

_____

_____

Mason couldn't decide whether to mindfully peel and eat an orange or eat chocolate. Eventually he decided on chocolate! He spent time thinking about the texture of the chocolate he was eating and paid attention to the crunch and softness of it melting in his mouth.

Mindful walking

Start by deciding where you're going to walk. This means you need a starting point and an end point. So, you could decide that your starting point is your front door and the end point is your local park or a friend's house.

Take a look at some Top Tips before you make a start.

- Mindful walking can be tricky because while walking there are multiple stimuli around us – for example, noises, smells and the things we see. We might even be interrupted by someone we know (or someone we don't!). That said, it's worth the effort because we spend so much time travelling that we have many opportunities to practise our mindfulness skills.

- We use the term mindful walking, but we can be mindful while using a wheelchair, rowing, sailing, running or swimming.

Mindful walking

When you've decided on where you're going to start and end your walk, go to the starting point.

1. As you start your walk, gently notice the different physical sensations in your body. Slow down slightly and pay attention to what this feels like. Now quicken your pace, noticing how this feels in contrast.

2. Spend some time noticing what you can see around you.

3. Notice what you can hear and then what you smell.

4. Notice what your feet come into contact with. For example, are you walking on grass or kicking through leaves?

5. What can you feel? Gently focus on what it feels like having the sun, rain or wind on your hair, face and hands as you're walking.

6. Zoom in and really pay attention to the sensations as first your heel touches the ground, notice what you feel in the middle part of your foot and how your toes feel as they touch the floor. Now focus on the sensations you feel as your heel lifts up before your next foot touches the floor. Gently focus on the process of walking. Be curious and spend some time noticing whether it's the left- or right-hand side of your foot that tends to make more contact with the ground.

7. Now zoom out – move the spotlight of your attention away from your bodily sensations and notice what you can see and hear in the far distance.

8. When you notice that your mind has moved to things that don't relate to the practice of mindful walking, appreciate that you've noticed this and gently bring your attention back to a particular focus.

When you have reached the end of your walk, spend some time reflecting on your experience of mindful walking.

What did you notice?

_____

_____

_____

Mason noticed that his left foot felt heavier as it touched the ground, Alex enjoyed the sensations of kicking through the leaves on the ground, Carter noticed that it was quite relaxing just to focus on mindful walking and Malia noticed that, once again, she started thinking about lunch but was able to refocus on the exercise!

You'll have started to appreciate that mindfulness really helps us pay attention in the present moment – the here and now. When we practise mindfulness we start to notice that our attention easily gets caught up by other things (a noise or a distracting thought), but the trick is to mindfully return our attention back to the task at hand.

Spend some more time reflecting on what you found useful in this chapter. What practice was helpful that you could try again?

_____

_____

_____

Could you put some time aside this week to practise a mindful activity? For example, could you go for a longer mindful walk, cook a whole meal while using mindfulness or brush your teeth mindfully? What would you like to try?

_____

_____

_____

My Kindness Box

So, thinking about what you've learnt in this chapter, what would you like to add to your Kindness Box? Would you like to add one of the mindfulness scripts or your reflections about mindful walking, mindful eating or mindful breathing or listening? Perhaps you could add a list of foods you would like to mindfully eat. How about including a note with the name of your favourite mindfulness practice to your Kindness Box? Could you make a bracelet that has different coloured beads and textures on it or keep a shiny stone in your pocket to remind you to focus on the _present_ moment (the gift of the here and now)?

Remember, your Kindness Box is a place that holds reminders of the things that boost your wellbeing. Focusing on photos of your favourite people, places or pets could help you practise mindfulness. You could put pamper products, your favourite lotion or a playlist of your favourite music in your box.

Summary

In this chapter, you have:

❖ Learnt that mindfulness involves paying attention to the present moment

❖ Mindfully focused on your breath and the sounds around you

❖ Explored how you can use mindfulness every day (e.g. mindful eating and walking)

❖ Considered additions to your Kindness Box

Additional notes

What will help me be kinder to myself?

What can I add to my Kindness Box?

6 The power of imagination

Our imagination can take us many places in our 'mind's eye'. We can imagine sitting on a peaceful, relaxing beach, scoring a goal for our favourite football team (in the last minute of extra time!), graduating from university or being in our favourite place, with our favourite people.

There is often an emphasis on the visual aspect of imagination, but imagery involves other senses too, such as sound, taste, smell and touch. We can use imagination to help us feel calm, psych ourselves up or help us slow down, all of which can have a positive impact on wellbeing. So, in this chapter you're going to use the *power of your imagination* to help give your wellbeing a boost.

In this chapter, you're going to:

- Imagine colours to help enhance wellbeing

- Use the power of your imagination to create a calming, peaceful, relaxing or soothing place in your mind

- Create an image of a Kindness Crusader, Cheerleader, Coach, Supportive Friend, Superhero and/or Compassionate Companion

- Think about what to add to your Kindness Box

Many people have found that using their imagination can unlock their potential and help give their confidence a boost. Imagery is used in many arenas such as sport, drama and art. Track athletes often engage with a visual 'film' (or a hopeful prediction) of their whole race prior to running it, footballers imagine, over and over, successful penalty kicks and tennis players their winning shots. This all occurs without a step taken, a football kicked or a tennis ball hit. It's all in their mind's eye, ear and (sometimes) nose and skin!

In recent years, scientists have found that the images we create in our minds can have a positive impact on our health and wellbeing. Did you know that when we create calm and peaceful images, our stress hormones reduce and our bodies slow down? Imagery actually stimulates the same part of our brain as real-life events do. For example, if we're really hungry and start to imagine what we're going to have for lunch our bodies will respond – our tummies may rumble. Just imagining the food leads to the exact same physiological response as actually having the plate of food in front of us.

Writers use the power of imagination to engage the reader, creatively encouraging us to imagine a scene. For example, when we're reading about the tales of Harry Potter, we are able to picture the scar on Harry's face, broomsticks, wizards, sorcerers and magic. We can imagine the smell and taste the flavour of the candy Harry and his friends eat on their train journey to Hogwarts, while our hearts race as we imagine a stomach-churning fall in Quidditch. All of this adds to our experience of reading, making it a full mind and body experience.

Different types of imagery

What do you notice when you try to visualise your route home from your local shop or imagine the layout of a classroom you once sat in (*visual imagery*)? Can you imagine the sound of your computer keyboard or your favourite song (*auditory imagery*)? What do you notice when you try to imagine the smell of your favourite food or perfume (*olfactory imagery*)? Can you imagine warm sand under your feet or the softness of your favourite blanket (*tactile imagery*)? If you think about your favourite meal, can you taste the flavour (*gustatory imagery*)?

You may have noticed that you didn't experience clear, HD visual pictures or hear your favourite singer as though you were streaming the track on your phone! But you probably experienced some form of images, sounds, smells, tastes and touch via your imagination.

Slowing and calming down our bodies

We're now going to focus on two imagery exercises that aim to soothe, calm and slow down our bodies. The first involves imagining a range of different colours with the aim of generating a calm and peaceful experience.  You may also discover a colour you're particularly drawn to and might benefit from imagining again and again in the future. The second exercise focuses on creating a calm, peaceful, soothing or relaxing place in your 'mind's eye'.

Research suggests that 1–3 per cent of the general population find it difficult, if not impossible, to generate or access visual imagery (it's called aphantasia). Therefore some people find sensing a colour is simpler than creating a place or a person in their mind's eye. Have a go at the different exercises and see if you have a preference.

Preparation for imagery exercises

Start the exercises by finding a place where you can sit without being disturbed – somewhere that's free from distractions. It's worth reading through each exercise first to familiarise yourself with the flow. It can help to sit on a chair in an upright position with your feet on the floor (shoulder-width apart) and your head also in an upright position. You can download recordings of the exercises at https://overcoming. co.uk/715/resources-to-download. If you're listening to the audio you can begin by gently closing your eyes; if you prefer to keep your eyes open focus your attention on something in front of you, such as the base of a picture frame or a mark on the floor.

Imagining colour

1. Once you've found somewhere to sit and have settled your mind and body, gently bring your attention to your breathing, becoming mindful of it. Notice the sensations as you breathe slowly in and then out. Feel your body begin to relax slightly as you breathe a little slower and deeper than usual. Let your shoulders drop and your jaw loosen.

2. When you're ready, create a picture in your mind of the colour blue. Imagine blue in all its different shades. You might picture the blue of the sky, or the sea, the blue of a soft blanket or a flower. You may simply prefer to imagine a block of colour. For a while, just enjoy the colour blue, allowing it to fill the entire visual field of your mind's eye.

3. Now allow the colour to change to orange in all its infinite possibilities. The orange of fresh fruit, flowers, vegetables, a warm jumper or a burning sunset. Allow yourself to enjoy the colour orange, noticing how you feel when you're appreciating it.

4. When you feel ready, allow the colour to change to red: a red landscape, roses, bricks or a luxurious rug. Imagine different tones and infinite possibilities. Immerse yourself in it.

5. When you're ready, allow the colour to change to yellow. Imagine the endless tones of the colour yellow, in all its various shades. The golden sun, daffodils, lemons and autumnal leaves. Imagine yellow close to you, far away or swirling around you.

6. Now let the colour you're imagining transition to green. Fill your imagination with the colour green, in all its shades. The green of grass, leaves, lush peapods, a dark forest or a wall of green paint. Imagine being surrounded by beautiful green in its many different tones. Enjoy the experience.

7. Allow the colour to change to violet. A beautiful sunset, flowers, a soft blanket or favourite toy from childhood. As you have done previously, immerse yourself in the colour and the experience.

8. Now allow your mind to move to other colours of your choosing. Maybe enjoying pinks, purples, browns . . .

9. When you're ready, notice how your mind and body feel. You may notice that your mind has slowed down and so has your body. Maybe one of the colours seemed to relax and calm you more than the others.

10. Is there a colour that suits you at the moment, one you wish to return to? Allow yourself a few minutes for the colour to return to you. Maybe bring a slight warmth to your facial expression or a slight smile to your mouth as you welcome it back. Experience the colour in all its brilliance and beauty.

With the knowledge that you can return to this exercise and experience these colours at any time, gently bring the exercise to a close and widen your awareness to the chair that's supporting you and the room that you're in. If your eyes have been closed, open them: lift your gaze. Take some calming breaths and maybe have a stretch before you write about what you noticed.

REFLECT

What did you notice? Did you find that a particular colour was calming or relaxing for you? Would it be helpful to repeat this exercise or parts of it?

_____

_____

_____

Mason noticed the colour yellow was really calming and returned to it at the end of the exercise, while Alex found the whole process of imagining colours and moving between them really relaxing. Carter found the colour red really exhilarating and his mind drifted off for a moment to his favourite football

team and their red kit. Malia recognised that for the first time in ages she wasn't preoccupied by her upcoming exams.

Creating a soothing place in your 'mind's eye'

EXPERIMENT

In this exercise, you're going to create an image of a place that makes you feel calm, peaceful, relaxed or soothed. Once again, you can choose to read through the script or, if you prefer, you can download the audio recording.

Have a look at the Top Tips box before you create your own soothing place.

TOP TIPS

- Before making a start, it can be helpful to think about how you want to refer to this place because the words you use can have a big impact on your experience. Some people like to use the term *'my safe place'* and feel this phrase evokes a helpful and wellbeing-boosting experience; for others the term *'my calm place'* or *'my peaceful place'* suits them better. How would you like to refer to this place? Maybe the term is unimportant or maybe it evolves and changes dependent upon what you need at the time – what is important is to find wording that's helpful for you.

Once you've decided what you want to call this place (that makes you feel calm, peaceful, content, relaxed or soothed) it can be helpful to make some notes about the kind of place you might wish to create for yourself.

 Where might your 'calming, peaceful, relaxing or soothing place' be? It could be a beach, your favourite spot in a park, a forest clearing or even your garden. If you're struggling to think of somewhere have a look at photos from holidays you've been on or look in magazines and on the internet for inspiration.

REFLECT

_____

_____

_____

What would you like to see, hear, touch and smell in this place? Maybe you want to hear the crash of ocean waves, a babbling stream or the whistling wind swirling round your favourite tree. Maybe you want to create a place where you can smell a perfume that's associated with fond memories, the fragrance of flowers or freshly cut grass. You may want to be able to touch something that's important to you or something that calms and soothes you.

Mason decided on his auntie's back garden; he liked to listen to the stream behind her house and the birds in the trees. Alex picked her local park because she liked to listen to the wind through the trees. Carter's calming place was a secluded beach he liked to visit with his family when he was on holiday. He could imagine the warm sun on his face and the soft sand under his feet. Malia imagined a room in her house, where she liked to read in front of a crackling log fire.

My calming, peaceful, relaxing or soothing place

1. Once you've found somewhere to sit and have settled your mind and body, gently bring your attention to your breathing, becoming mindful of it. Notice the sensations as you breathe slowly in and slowly out. Feel your body begin to relax slightly as you breathe a little slower and deeper than usual. Let your shoulders drop and your jaw loosen.

2. Allow an image to form that's calming, peaceful, relaxing or soothing in some way. You may have been to this place, but it doesn't matter if you haven't – it can be somewhere you've created in your mind or that you've seen in magazines or on TV.

3. Don't worry if no image comes to mind straightaway. Just gently try to allow an image to form that's special to you.

4. When your mind has settled on an image, spend a couple of minutes paying attention to what you can see.

5. Now spend some time noticing what you can hear in your special place. Notice the different qualities of the sounds and how they make you feel.

6. Are there any soothing or comforting smells present?

7. Spend some time noticing any physical sensations. Is there anything in your image that you want to touch? You may wish to feel sand, super-soft carpet, water or grass under your feet. You may notice the warmth of the sun on your face or a gentle breeze blowing through your hair.

8. Now notice whether you're on your own in your calming, peaceful, relaxing or soothing place. Would you like to have somebody or something (perhaps an animal) with you?

9. Imagine that this place has an awareness of you. For a few moments, just imagine that the place you have chosen is really

delighted to see you. How does it feel to know that this is your very own place and its only purpose is to help and support you?

10. Is there anything else you would like to do? You may just want to be still, or you may imagine you're walking or swimming. You may want to have fun on a swing, play a game or just relax in a hammock. This is your special place and you can use it in any way that helps you to feel at ease.

With the knowledge that you can return to this exercise and experience your calming, peaceful, relaxing or soothing place at any time, gently bring the exercise to a close and widen your awareness to the chair that's supporting you and the room that you're in. If your eyes have been closed, open them: lift your gaze. Take some calming breaths and maybe have a stretch before you write about what you noticed.

How did it feel creating your own calming, peaceful, relaxing or soothing place? What could you see, smell and touch? How did it feel knowing that this special place was there just to support you?

_____

_____

_____

Carter noticed that his mind wandered at one point but reminded himself that this was OK because that's what minds sometimes do! Thinking about his calming place, the sand under his feet and sun on his face made him feel relaxed. 'I feel like I'm on holiday again,' he thought to himself and felt happy knowing that he could return to his calming place any time.

It can be helpful to put some time aside in the coming days to repeat the exercise. Have a look at the Top Tips section and see if you can experiment with your calming, peaceful, relaxing or soothing place further.

- Some people find background music helps them. Perhaps experiment and see if music helps you connect even more with your calming, peaceful, relaxing or soothing place.

- Some people like to hold an object that helps them feel soothed. See if holding something helps you. It could be a photograph, a soft, cuddly, teddy bear or a shiny stone that somebody has given you.

Building a team around you

Did you know our brain and body respond to a *generated image* or *sense* of someone being kind to us, in almost the same way as it does if a real person was actually there? Of course, there's nothing like feeling supported by another person or getting a hug from a friend or family member, but sometimes it's useful to use our imagination when we're in need of a boost.

Research shows that imaginary friends and companions are a normal part of childhood (and even adulthood for many of us). Commonly they take human form, but sometimes the images are animals, angels or toys. Imaginary friends often take on the characteristics of something we need that we think will help us. They usually 'disappear' when we become more self-aware and preoccupied with the opinions of others who we think might see it as 'childish'. Researchers have found that fiction writers are more likely to have had imaginary companions as children, which suggests that they are associated with creativity.

In this next exercise (which is one of our favourites), you're going to create an image of someone or something (maybe an animal, the ocean, an old oak tree with solid roots or a mountain) that is kind, compassionate and supportive and has your wellbeing and best interests at heart.

Take a moment to consider what kind of support you might benefit from right now. Imagine someone or something that would have a calming effect on you, cheer you on or reassure you. What qualities would they have? What might they look like? Where might they be in relation to you? If they spoke what might their tone of voice be like? How would their facial expression and voice tone show that they care for and support you?

_____

_____

_____

_____

_____

You may choose to call this image your Kindness Crusader, Cheerleader, Coach, Supportive Friend, Superhero and/or Compassionate Companion. What's important to remember is that this image has your best interests at heart and is something that can help you feel cared for and supported. Have a look at our Kindness Crusaders for inspiration!

My kind, supportive image

Find somewhere comfortable to sit where you'll not be disturbed. Once you've settled your mind and body, gently bring your attention to your breathing, becoming mindful of it. Notice the sensations as you breathe slowly in and out. Feel your body begin to relax slightly as you breathe a little slower and deeper than usual. Let your shoulders drop and your jaw loosen. Lower your gaze and if you're listening to the audio (and if it's comfortable to do so), close your eyes.

1. Imagine sitting in the presence of someone or something that is infinitely supportive of you.

2. Spend some time thinking about what the image looks like. If it helps think about different images and options before you settle on one.

3. Imagine this image has your best interests at heart; they are non-judgemental and have your wellbeing first and foremost in their mind.

4. They know how difficult life is for you and they possess the exact qualities you need, at this very moment. They're supportive, kind, encouraging, calming and/or empowering. You may notice that they want to encourage, not judge you, and they want you to flourish.

5. Where would you like them to be in relation to you? Maybe in front of you or at your side?

6. If your image has a face, what does their facial expression look like? If your image has a voice, what does their voice sound like? What might they say to you that shows they care for you and support you?

7. Allow a slight smile to arrive on your face as you experience their warmth, compassion and kindness. You may feel comforted or strengthened by their support.

8.   Now spend a few minutes simply sitting in their presence and allow yourself to feel the care and support they're offering you.

9.   Is there anything they want you to know or you want to hear?

When you're ready, with the knowledge that you can return to this exercise at any time, gently bring it to a close and widen your awareness to the chair that's supporting you and the room that you're in. If your eyes have been closed, open them: lift your gaze. Take some calming breaths and maybe have a stretch before you write about what you noticed.

How did it feel focusing on an image of someone or something that cares for you? Perhaps it was like being in the presence of a kind, supportive friend? How did it feel knowing they had your best interests at heart, that they were there just for you?

_____

_____

_____

_____

Mason created an image of his own Kindness Crusader. He found it helpful to think of his image as his kind and supportive guide. Alex didn't settle on an image but had a strong sense of a golden light. It made her feel strong and empowered. Carter imagined an old, wiser version of himself. This was comforting to him as it gave him a sense that all would be OK. He smiled as he named it 'wise Carter'. Malia experienced a strong sense of someone being at her side, their hand on her shoulder. 'You can do this,' she heard being whispered and thought it sounded like her grandma. It gave her strength for her psychology exam the next day.

TOP TIPS

- Having experienced the exercise consider how you might want to refer to this part of you that's supportive and kind.

- Why stop here? How about returning to this exercise when you're in need of some courage or encouragement? If you were a cat, you might channel your inner lion! Could you try the exercise again, perhaps when you've had a great day and also on a day when you're upset, angry or anxious? It might help to build a team around you – or someone with whom you can let off steam, safe in the knowledge they will not judge you.

- In Philip Pullman's book series 'His Dark Materials', characters each have a 'Dæmon' or animal that's external to them and represents their 'inner-self'. Dæmons are intelligent and independent, helping their 'humans' achieve goals in life and sometimes they have fun along the way – how about creating the image of a Dæmon to be of assistance to you?

Before you move on to the chapter summary, spend some time reflecting on what you found useful in this chapter. What practice was helpful that you could try again?

REFLECT

_____

_____

_____

_____

My Kindness Box

Before you move on to Part 3 spend some time considering what you would like to add to your Kindness Box. You may decide to draw a picture of your calming, peaceful, relaxing or soothing place. You could add the image you created (of another person, animal or part of nature) that cares for and supports you. You may choose to add a photo or a copy of the script for your calming, peaceful, relaxing or soothing place. Just like building up muscle by going to the gym, you're giving your wellbeing a boost by working through the exercises in the book.

Summary

In this chapter, you have:

❖ Learnt that imagery stimulates the same part of your brain as real-life events do

❖ Imagined colours to enhance your wellbeing

❖ Used the power of imagination to create a calming, peaceful, relaxing or soothing place

❖ Generated an image of a Kindness Crusader, Cheerleader, Coach, Supportive Friend, Superhero and/or Compassionate Companion. You may have even created a Dæmon!

❖ Considered what you would like to add to your Kindness Box

Additional notes

What will help me be kinder to myself?

What can I add to my Kindness Box?

Part 3

THE FABULOUS FOUR – PHYSIOLOGY, FEELINGS, THOUGHTS AND BEHAVIOUR

There are eight chapters in this section, focusing on physiology (our body, its functions and physical sensations), feelings, thoughts and behaviour. In Part 3 we have settled on some commonly used terms, but you might prefer to use different words to describe your experiences. For example, you might refer to emotions rather than feelings, or actions rather than behaviours. All four (physiology, feelings, thoughts and behaviour) are important aspects of our lives and interact with each other.

Before we look at each area in more detail, let's take a look at a situation Jess found herself in. This will help set the scene as you move through the chapters.

Jess received a text from her best friend to say they had been invited to a New Year's Eve party. On receiving the invite, Jess immediately felt a sudden wave of anxiety and began to worry.

Let's have a look at the different aspects of her experience:

- **Physiology** Heart racing, feeling sick and a loss of appetite

- **Feelings** Anxious and a little fearful

- **Thoughts** 'Oh no, what if I don't know what to say to people when I get there?', 'What if I stutter or blush when I'm spoken to?', 'I want to go because I don't want to miss out . . . but what if no one likes me?'

- **Behaviour** Frozen to the spot, as though time stood still, quickly followed by the urge to make an excuse and stay at home

We can see in the diagram below the interaction between 'the fabulous four'.

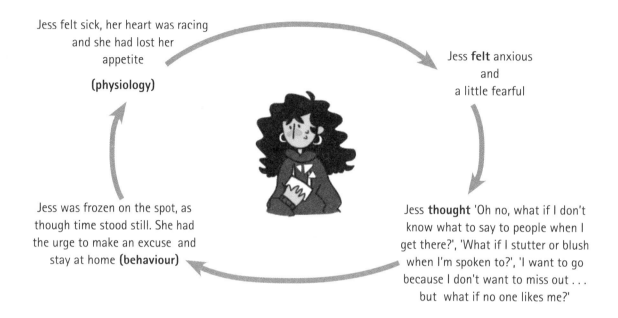

Jess felt sick, her heart was racing and she had lost her appetite
(physiology)

Jess **felt** anxious and a little fearful

Jess was frozen on the spot, as though time stood still. She had the urge to make an excuse and stay at home **(behaviour)**

Jess **thought** 'Oh no, what if I don't know what to say to people when I get there?', 'What if I stutter or blush when I'm spoken to?', 'I want to go because I don't want to miss out . . . but what if no one likes me?'

When we're not feeling our best, focusing on each separate but related area can give us great ideas about how we can boost our wellbeing. This is what the following chapters are all about, discovering techniques and strategies to help you get the most out of life.

In Part 3, a number of new characters will also join us. You'll be introduced to AJ, Katrina, Ella, Tyler, Bilal, Jess, Chloe, Yuan and Nina, whose stories will bring the exercises to life!

7 Nourishing and nurturing your body and yourself

There are many things you can't control about your body. Your fingernails will always grow, the lining of your stomach replaces itself frequently and the outer layer of your skin drops off – everywhere! However, there are some important things you can control that have a *BIG* impact on your wellbeing. So, this chapter is here to inspire you to make positive changes by nourishing and nurturing your body. After all, we can all do with a 'reset' from time to time.

In this chapter, you're going to:

- Explore how diet, exercise and sleep can impact on wellbeing

- Have a go at Progressive Muscle Relaxation

- Negotiate obstacles with kindness

- Consider additional changes you can make that are unique to you

- Create a Healthy Me Vision Board to inspire and motivate you

- Think about what to add to your Kindness Box

Nourishing your body (and mind)

In Chapter 1 we examined the relationship between physical and mental health and focused on how they influence each other. If we feel physically healthy, this can have a positive impact on wellbeing and if we feel mentally well, this can boost our physical health. In this chapter, we'll explore how we can boost both our mental and physical health by focusing on diet, activity and sleep patterns. Small changes in these areas can really help.

Let's take a closer look at how certain food and drinks can influence wellbeing.

- A lack of certain vitamins and blood sugar lows and highs have been found to be associated with a whole range of symptoms including fatigue, irritability, concentration problems, anxiety and low mood

- Specific foods and drinks have been found to affect sleep; although alcohol or drugs might make you feel sleepy, they affect the quality of your sleep

- The impact of caffeine is well documented and is found in tea, coffee and – of course – chocolate!

Developing your 'Nourishment Recipe'

A good starting point is to think about whether there has been a specific time in your life when you had a healthier diet. Your body doesn't need to have been a temple, but maybe you were just a bit healthier. You may have been the orchestrator of your healthy diet (deciding what you ate and drank) or it might have been the result of other factors (such as living at home with your parents, being on holiday or signed up to a healthy boot camp!).

- Nourishing yourself doesn't mean never having things you really fancy. Instead, it's about seeking balance and ultimately a healthier and happier you.

- Much of what is written about diets is based on losing weight, avoiding 'danger' or 'bad' foods and 'sins'. We're told to 'battle' our urges and deprive ourselves. It can be helpful to reclaim the word 'diet' (which simply means the kind of food we eat) and focus on nourishing ourselves, motivated by kindness.

- Put 'Yorkshire Pudding' into any search engine and you'll find lots of different recipes. Different ratios of eggs, flour and milk, different types of oil, oven temperatures and even recommended additions (such as cinnamon!). The point we're trying to make is that your nourishment plan is likely to contain core ingredients, but the way you use them is likely to be specific to you.

Start by completing the Nourishment Worksheet below, making note of what might be helpful to continue to do, reintroduce and to try. Once you've completed the worksheet think about the potential personal benefits of your plan. Use words and/or draw simple pictures in the space provided to capture what comes to mind. Before you start, take a look at AJ's story and his completed worksheet.

AJ had moved away from his parents' home (and cooking) and although there were many positives to this, his diet, exercise routine and sleep patterns had taken a nose-dive. While socialising he was drinking more alcohol and eating quite a lot of take-away foods. He didn't prioritise exercise as much as he used to and found his energy levels were lower. AJ decided to make some changes.

AJ's Nourishment Worksheet

Nourishment	Things I used to do and want to continue	New ideas/things to try
Eating	I had fewer snacks I ate more vegetables I had smaller portion sizes I didn't eat on the go I planned meals in advance I didn't eat on auto-pilot	I want to be more 'mindful' when I'm eating I'd like to try different recipes and vegetarian options
Drinking	I drank more water and had alcohol-free nights each week	I'd like to try a reusable bottle because it's good for the environment and it will encourage me to drink more water

Personal benefits I'm likely to achieve

I'll feel happier and healthier
I'm likely to have more energy and find it easier to make some other changes too

My Nourishment Worksheet

Nourishment	Things I used to do and want to continue	New ideas / things to try
Eating		
Drinking		
Personal benefits I'm likely to achieve		

Nurturing your body and mind through activity

It's likely you already know about some of the benefits of physical activity, so in this section you're going to consider how to give your wellbeing a boost through physical exercise. Again it can help to consider what you've done in the past, new things to try and the potential personal benefits you'll experience due to the changes you intend to make.

- It's worth noting that while some people might benefit from *more* physical activity others might benefit from *less*! You might find it helpful to simply change something you already do. For example, join a group instead of exercising on your own, do an activity at the start or end of your day or maybe practise some yoga in your room (instead of only doing the downward dog during a yoga class!).

Take a look at AJ's Activity Plan – and then have a go at completing your own.

AJ's Activity Plan

Activities to reintroduce	Activities to try
Go out on my bike more often instead of using the car Use the stairs instead of the lift Go for a swim twice a week	Ask my brother if he can teach me how to play squash Look at YouTube and try out some fitness classes Join a five-a-side football team
Personal benefits I'm likely to achieve	
I'll feel fitter and be more confident I'll have MORE ENERGY I'm likely to be happier!	

Now it's your turn. What makes it into your Activity Plan?

My Activity Plan

Activities to reintroduce	Activities to try

Personal benefits I'm likely to achieve

Potential blocks

Sometimes things can get in the way of us engaging in healthy levels of exercise. For example, we may:

- Think other people will judge us

- Talk ourselves down or out of doing the activity because we feel we have to be amazing at it (especially if we're on public view)

- Be concerned about body image issues

- Have physical health difficulties

- Lack motivation

- Feel we don't have the time to fit it into our already busy life

If any of these blocks apply to you, consider how you might overcome them and/or discuss them with someone whose opinion you value. Could you do the activity with a friend or family member? Would putting a reminder on your phone (to prompt you to do an activity) be helpful? Later in the book we will also give you some ideas about how to overcome common blocks (for example, in Chapters 12 and 13 we explore how you can prepare for change and boost the probability of success).

Now, let's turn our attention to sleep, as a lack of it (or even too much) can also have an impact on wellbeing.

Restoring your body (and mind) . . . ZZZZZZZ . . .

A lack of sleep can sometimes, in the short term, make us feel quite buzzy (especially if there's a good reason for our sleep deprivation), but for most of us and in the majority of situations, a lack of sleep has a negative impact on our wellbeing. It's associated with higher levels of anxiety, lower mood, difficulty concentrating and memory issues. Alternatively, a good night's sleep allows our body to repair, while our brain weeds out what it doesn't need, consolidates what it does need and processes a whole load of important 'stuff'.

- Did you know humans are the only mammals who willingly delay sleep?

- People who don't get enough sleep are more likely to have bigger appetites as their leptin levels (an appetite-regulating hormone) fall, promoting appetite increase

- Lights and alarms that simulate sunset and sunrise have been found to help people get a good night's sleep, as well as assisting those who experience Seasonal Affective Disorder (SAD); some alarms also play a choice of natural noises, such as crashing waves or chirping birds

- Melatonin is produced in our brain when light levels are low to promote sleep, so consider switching your gadgets to night mode late at night

If you do struggle with sleep, or simply want some ideas for a better night's sleep, have a look at some Top Tips.

TOP TIPS

- A good starting point is to think about specific times in your life when your sleep has been good and consider the conditions that contributed to this. You may not have been jumping out of bed 100 per cent refreshed and ready for the day ahead, but hopefully you can think of a time when you had a better night's sleep.

- Retiring to a cool room after a warm bath or shower is a good bedtime routine that many people find useful.

- Gaming and pinging phones just before bed are just some of the screen-associated activities that can make it difficult to sleep. It's not about depriving yourself of things that are important to you, but being mindful of what is and isn't helpful just before bedtime.

- Exercise can help you get a good night's sleep – but make sure it's not just before you go to bed as this can make you buzzy rather than sleepy.

- Music, a warm light, black-out blinds, a book to read and relax with, sleep masks, ear plugs and calming scent are just some of the *additions* people use to get a better night's sleep. Switching off notifications, removing devices and 'work' from the bedroom can be helpful *subtractions.*

- It's helpful to consider the benefits you're likely to experience by improving your sleep. Some people find it helpful to write a 'to do list' before going to bed. This helps decrease the likelihood of thoughts relating to *'jobs to do tomorrow'* whirling round in your head, preventing sleep.

If sleep is something you want to improve, have a go at creating a Sleep Plan. Have a look at AJ's Sleep Plan for some ideas before you create your own.

AJ's Sleep Plan

Things that have helped me get a good night's sleep in the past	Exercises from The Kindness Workbook that could help	New ideas to try
Turning screens off 30 minutes or so before bed so I'm not tempted to check notifications just before sleep	The Mindful Breathing exercise in chapter 5 could help	Getting a black-out blind
Putting my phone on silent	The Calm and Peaceful place exercise in chapter 6 could help	Having soft lighting in the bedroom
Not eating or drinking too much fluid just before bed		Doing a relaxation exercise just before bed
Having a glass of water at the side of my bed	I'll use both exercises to help me drift off to sleep and when I wake up in the night	Playing some relaxing music
Being more active during the day		
Not drinking alcohol every night		

Personal benefits I'm likely to achieve
I'd be more alert I'd make better decisions I'd be happier (less grumpy!) and healthier

My Sleep Plan

Things that have helped me get a good night's sleep in the past	Exercises from The Kindness Workbook that could help	New ideas to try

Personal benefits I'm likely to achieve

Progressive Muscle Relaxation (PMR)

This exercise helps gradually wind down your body and mind. It involves slowly tensing and relaxing different muscle groups in turn. Although PMR can provide almost immediate relaxation for some, the accumulative effect of frequent practice is particularly helpful for our wellbeing. With experience, you'll become more aware of when you're not relaxed, you'll notice when you're tense or on edge and you'll then be able to use this exercise to assist you. If you have any injuries or pain you can skip those affected areas, keeping in mind throughout the exercise the importance of tension without straining yourself.

Start by finding somewhere you can sit comfortably where you will not be disturbed for around 10–15 minutes. Alternatively, you might prefer to lie down.

Progressive Muscle Relaxation

1. Gently close your eyes, or if you're reading the script (rather than listening to an audio), try and focus your attention on something in front of you, such as the base of a picture frame or a mark on the floor. Notice how your mind and body feel as you begin the exercise. Simply notice how you are in this present moment.

2. Begin by taking a smooth, slow, deep breath in, noticing the feeling of air filling your lungs. Hold your breath for a few seconds. Now release the breath slowly from your mouth or nose and let tension leave your body.

3. When ready, take another smooth, slow, deep breath in. Again, slowly release your breath, allowing tension to leave your body.

4. Even slower now, take another breath, fill your lungs and hold the air. Once again, slowly release the breath and imagine the feeling of tension leaving your body.

5. Now move your attention to your feet. Begin to tense your feet by curling your toes and arches. Hold on to the tension, noticing what it feels like (pause for 5 seconds). Then release the tension from your feet, noticing the feeling of relaxation.

6. Now bring your attention to your lower legs. Tense the muscles in your calves. Hold them tightly, noticing the feeling of tension.

Pause for 5 seconds and then release the tension from your lower legs, noticing the feeling of relaxation.

7. Now tense the muscles of your upper legs and pelvis, maybe squeezing your thighs together and clenching your buttocks. Notice the feeling of tension this creates. Pause for 5 seconds and then release, feeling the tension leaving your muscles.

8. Begin to tense the muscles of your stomach and chest. Hold the tension, noticing the sensation. Once again, hold for 5 seconds and then release, noticing the feeling of relaxation.

9. Now tense the muscles in your back, maybe focusing on your shoulder blades. Notice the feeling of tension, holding onto it for 5 seconds before gently letting go, allowing your back to relax.

10. Tense your arms, all the way from your fingertips to your shoulders. Make a fist and squeeze all the way up your arm, noticing the tension. Once again, hold for around 5 seconds. Release the tension in your hands, arms and shoulders, noticing the sensation of relaxation.

11. Raise your shoulders up towards your ears for about 5 seconds, noticing the tension this creates. Now relax your shoulders, allowing them to lower slowly, noticing the sensation of relaxation as you do so.

12. Tense your face and neck, maybe furrowing your brow, tensing your lips and pushing your tongue against the roof of your mouth. Hold the tension once again for around 5 seconds and then relax your face and neck, noticing the sensation of relaxation.

13. Finally tense your whole body. Your feet, calves, thighs, pelvis, stomach, chest, arms, back, head and neck. Notice the tension throughout your body. Hold once again for around 5 seconds and then release, allowing your whole body to relax.

With the knowledge that you can return to this exercise at any time, gently bring the exercise to a close and widen your awareness to whatever is supporting you and the room that you're in.

REFLECT

What did you notice? Did you notice the difference between the tense and relaxed states? Would it be helpful to repeat this exercise before sleep? Is there anything you might add to or adjust in the exercise? For example, would background music, a comfy blanket or a relaxing scent such as lavender help you to relax?

_____

_____

_____

Extending the theme of nourishing and nurturing your body

In this chapter, you've reflected on how your diet, day-to-day activities and sleep patterns help 'nourish and nurture' your body, and you've also tried PMR. We're now going to ask you to extend these ideas further.

Have you been putting off or avoiding something? Perhaps you've been avoiding going to the dentist, visiting your GP, cutting your toenails or having your hair cut. Perhaps you're

not walking your dog or connecting with nature as much as you would like to. Nurturing and nourishing your body could involve moisturising your skin or buying some comfortable shoes.

Let's have a look at AJ's worksheet, which focuses on additional ideas that may give his wellbeing a boost. When you're ready, have a go at completing your own.

AJ's Boosting My Wellbeing Worksheet

Additional ideas to give my wellbeing a boost
Book a check-up at the dentist – and don't cancel it!
Get a shave
Make an appointment with my GP to speak about my acne and see if they can recommend anything or refer me to see someone about it

Personal benefits I'm likely to achieve
If I prioritise my health I'll feel better because I won't have that nagging voice in my head saying 'why aren't you doing x, y and z'
There might be something I can do about my acne
I'll feel better and more confident if I take more pride in my appearance

Boosting My Wellbeing Worksheet

Additional ideas to give my wellbeing a boost
Personal benefits I'm likely to achieve

So how exactly do you make all of the above happen? Let's take a look!

Motivating and supporting yourself with kindness

It's easy to be self-critical when we fall short of what we want for ourselves. It's also easy to throw in the towel and think *'I'm giving up for the rest of the day, now anything goes'.* So, having considered the changes you might want to make, let's consider how kindness can help when you have a setback.

Imagine a friend is trying to adopt a healthier lifestyle. They've had a week of stress and setbacks. They realise that the choices they have made were not healthy ones. They feel sluggish and down on themselves. What might you say to them and what tone of voice might you use? Would you criticise them or would you be supportive and kind to them? How would you show kindness and care to them? What encouragement and support would you give them?

_____

_____

_____

Think about how you could be that supportive and kind friend to yourself. What could you say to yourself when *you* have a setback? What would help you move forward? If you were speaking to yourself, what tone of voice could you use? You could use the space below to write some notes or alternatively write a supportive note or letter to yourself. If it helps use emojis to remind yourself of the tone of voice it would be good to use. Have a look at AJ's letter as an example.

_____

_____

_____

AJ wrote:

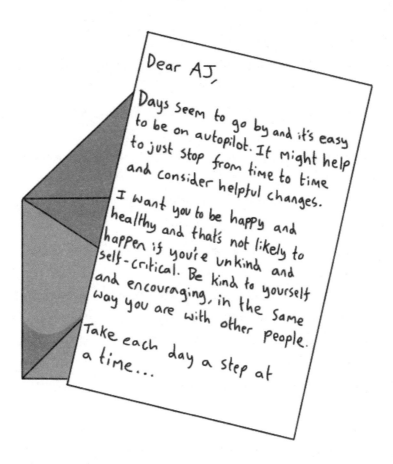

Dear AJ,

Days seem to go by and it's easy to be on autopilot. It might help to just stop from time to time and consider helpful changes. I want you to be happy and healthy and that's not likely to happen if you're unkind and self-critical. Be kind to yourself and encouraging, in the same way you are with other people. Take each day a step at a time...

TOP TIPS

- Problem-solving skills (thinking about what would be helpful for you to do and what the benefits would be) are a great way to make change more likely. So, if you've been putting off going to the doctor, could a friend go with you? If you want to nourish your skin, would it help to have moisturiser at the side of your bed to act as a reminder? If you want to do more exercise, would it help if your gym shoes were by your front door?

REMEMBER

Nourishing and nurturing your body isn't the product of a day, a week or even a month. It's not demolished by a given period of time, a meal, a holiday or a night out. Focus on working towards a healthier you, step by step. All you need to do today is take a step in the direction you want to travel.

Creating a Healthy Me Vision Board

A Healthy Me Vision Board is a great way to motivate and inspire you to make helpful choices. It turns up the dial of creativity, generating an eye-catching visual you can hang on your wall, have as a screensaver and/or place in your Kindness Box. Have a look at AJ's vision board for inspiration and then have a go at creating your own.

Start by considering what you want to make your vision board from. You might source a large piece of cardboard, a piece of paper, a polystyrene sheet or flat piece of wood. You might even go 3D creative or generate a digital image.

Using ideas from the worksheets you've completed in the chapter, add photos, images and drawings of nourishing food and drinks, activities you would like to try and things that help you get a good night's sleep. For example, you might include pictures of activities relating to a new sport you'd like to try, a gym you'd like to join, images relating to a good night's sleep, or of special treats that you might have occasionally that can help grab your attention, while also making your mouth water! How about adding reminders of exercises from *The Kindness Workbook* that may help improve your sleep? For example, focusing on a picture of a beach, ancient woodland or amazing skyline may trigger a memory of your 'calming, peaceful, relaxing or soothing place' just before bedtime. Perhaps have a sketch of your supportive Kindness Crusader on your vision board as a reminder that they have your best interests at heart.

AJ cut images from magazines of luscious meals with amazing, colourful salads and he also asked his dad for some recipes, which he clipped to his vision board. He found a local gym that he wanted to join so that he could spend some time focusing on his physical health. AJ also added statements of encouragement and support that he knew would help him if he had a setback, and a prompt to remind himself to use a kind and caring voice tone when he said the statements to himself.

My Kindness Box

It's time to consider what this chapter might inspire you to put in your Kindness Box. You could write a 'Future Me' letter letting the 'Future You' know what you wish for them and how focusing on your physical health may be worth considering. Pick a point in time, maybe a month, year or decade away and write to yourself, with kindness, considering what you can do to help now and in the future. You might choose to write or print the letter. Adding mouth-watering, healthy recipe cards to your Kindness Box may serve to remind you to be kind by fuelling your body with healthy meals or snacks. Adding a copy of your Healthy Me Vision Board or taking a photograph of it on your phone may also act as a prompt to be 'kinder to yourself'.

Summary

In this chapter, you have:

❖ Explored how diet, sleep and physical activity influence wellbeing

❖ Focused on tensing and relaxing muscles

❖ Employed kindness to negotiate obstacles

❖ Considered additional changes that are unique to you

❖ Created a Healthy Me Vision Board

❖ Considered what you would like to add to your Kindness Box

Additional notes

What will help me be kinder to myself?

What can I add to my Kindness Box?

8 Getting your body on board

Ever had well-meaning advice? Maybe you could see the logic behind the advice, but found it difficult to put it into practice? If this is the case, you're not on your own. Although there's no single magic answer as to how to put all this advice into practice, we certainly know a number of **body-focused** tricks that might be of assistance. Implementing these ideas into your daily life can be an act of kindness towards yourself.

In this chapter, you're going to:

- Consider how your body posture, movements, facial expression and breathing can change dependent upon how you're feeling

- Explore how you can use your breath to help calm both your body and mind

- Use 'method acting' to give yourself a helping hand

- Think about what to add to your Kindness Box

Your body is the 'place' from which your *thoughts* and *feelings* emerge. Just as we need to look after plants for them to flower, it helps to nurture and pay attention to our bodies, so we can flourish. Let's have a look at how to do that.

Body posture, movements, facial expression and breathing

Have you noticed your feelings are associated with subtle, and not so subtle, changes in your body posture, movements, facial expression and breathing? What about 'reading' other people? Are you good at noticing if someone is feeling happy, low or anxious? If so, you're likely to be picking up signals from their body, facial expression and breathing.

Body language is a type of non-verbal communication, which includes posture, movements of the body and eyes, gestures, facial expressions, breathing and use of space. Social psychologists have spent decades studying what our body language communicates to other people. Amazingly, they have found that our own body language affects our physiology and our wellbeing too. So, walking tall can *literally* make you feel more confident!

It's not just body language that can influence how we feel. We've known for a long time that different situations affect our breathing. We breathe slower when we're relaxed, while in situations that trigger 'fight or flight' our breathing rate increases, helping our body prepare for imminent danger. The latter is very helpful when there's something we need to react to, but it's a terrible strategy if we're in an exam, interview or on a date!

Importantly scientists have found that consciously slowing down our breathing can have a positive impact on our physiology, brain functioning and wellbeing. So focusing on our breathing can be a *really* important skill to learn.

All these insights are used by actors, athletes and musicians in order to enhance both their wellbeing and performance. For example, actors use their body posture, movements, facial expression and breathing as a way to 'get into the shoes' of the character they wish to portray.

How feelings influence us physically

We can all recognise the following physical reactions:

- When *anxious* our muscles tense, our fists may clench, our facial expression stiffens, we may chew our lip or frown and our breathing becomes fast and shallow

- When *happy* our body language tends to be open, we may jump for joy, smile, throw our arms in the air and our breathing might quicken

- When *relaxed* our shoulders drop, our facial expression appears calm and our breathing is slow, deep and steady

We're going to focus on feelings in more detail in Chapters 9 and 10, but in this next section we'll have a look at how different feelings affect our body posture, movements, facial expression and breathing. Writing about your insights can give you more awareness and – importantly – a source of material to help 'get your body on board' and improve your wellbeing. Have a look at the Top Tips box for a few additional ideas before you make a start.

- If you find it difficult to imagine specific situations, it might be useful to look through some family photos and recall how you were feeling at the time. Notice your facial expression and how you were holding your body.

- As you imagine a situation you may notice your body posture, movements, facial expression and breathing changes in the here and now. This is further information about how feelings affect you.

- As you work through the exercises you might notice other things. For example, different feelings might evoke gestures, eye movements and changes in jaw tension. These are all great insights so don't feel you have to restrict yourself to the prompts written.

- At set points during the exercise, you'll be prompted to take a few calming breaths to help settle your mind and body. If you find this tricky, or want a bit more guidance, skip back to the Mindfulness and/or Imagery Chapters (5 and 6) in Part 2 (Building Blocks for Everyday Life) to remind yourself of the exercises.

Imagine you're **anxious**, **worried** or **afraid** (maybe about an exam or a job interview). Perhaps you can imagine meeting someone new or finding yourself up a set of ladders (not at the same time though!). How could this affect your body posture, movements, facial expression and breathing?

Take some calming breaths and allow the image to fade from your mind and body.

Now, imagine you're feeling **down** or **sad** (maybe you performed badly at an interview, had a falling out with a friend or suffered a relationship break up). How could this affect your body posture, movements, facial expression and breathing?

Take some calming breaths and allow the image to fade from your mind and body.

Imagine you're feeling really **happy**, **confident** or **carefree** (maybe you passed a test, were having fun on holiday or celebrating a birthday with family or friends). How could this affect your body posture, movements, facial expression and breathing?

Take some calming breaths and allow the image to fade from your mind and body.

Now imagine you're feeling **irritable**, **angry** or **frustrated** (maybe someone pulled out in front of you when you were driving, accused you of something you didn't do, or your team lost an important match in the last moments of the game). How could this affect your body posture, movements, facial expression and breathing?

_____

_____

_____

Take some calming breaths and allow the image to fade from your mind and body.

Finally, imagine you're really **relaxed** (maybe after a massage, relaxation exercise or catnap on holiday). How could this affect your body posture, movements, facial expression and breathing?

_____

_____

_____

Take some calming breaths and allow the image to fade from your mind and body.

Experimenting with your body

Knowing how your body responds when you feel a certain way is a great insight – but how about using that insight to enhance your wellbeing?

Having discovered how your body posture, movements, facial expression and breathing changes in different situations, let's be playful by reversing *cause and effect*. In other words, consciously change each of these elements, and notice what impact this has on you.

When your posture slumps or becomes tense, this affects your breathing rate and lung capacity in a way that's not so great for your wellbeing. In contrast, relaxing, rolling your shoulders back and opening your chest gives your lungs plenty of room to breathe.

In the next exercise, have a go at intentionally altering your body posture, movements, facial expression and breathing. As you engage with each example provided, notice how you feel. It might help to stretch or engage in a calming exercise between each one. There's space provided for you to make note of your insights.

Body posture and movements

- Roll your shoulders back and walk with eyes towards the skyline
- Roll your shoulders forward, eyes on the ground
- Make your hands into fists
- Expand your arms out wide

_____

_____

_____

_____

Facial expression

- Consciously scrunch up your face

- Furrow your brow

- Bring a slight smile to your face

Breathing

- Breathe faster for a short length of time

- Gently slow down your breathing

- Breathe for a couple of seconds in a jerky way

- Breathe smooooothly . . .

TOP TIPS

- Feeling 100 per cent confident in an anxiety-provoking situation might be a stretch too far, but making small adjustments to your body posture, movements, facial expression and breathing will help you feel a bit more confident and can be very useful.

Although you might find it relatively simple to adjust your body posture, movements and facial expression, it may be trickier to alter your breathing rate. So let's take a closer look at breathing and then have a go at an exercise that aims to help calm and slow your body down.

Learning to use breathing to your advantage

Throughout the course of our lives, breathing is a constant – something most of us do automatically and without much thought. Bringing attention to the breath can create an amazing sense of steadiness – like the stability an anchor gives a boat. We can train ourselves to have more conscious control over our breathing and, by doing so, have more control over our physiology and brain function. Learning to breathe **smoothly**, **calmly and rhythmically** can significantly help to calm us down *and* keep us calm.

Simple breathing practices that slow our bodies down have been found to improve Heart Rate Variability (HRV) while also improving creativity, cognitive processes (such as memory and concentration), energy levels and decision making.

A slow breathing rate for one person might be quick for another. For example, until we're 12 months old, breathing rates are reported to average anywhere between 30–60 breaths per minute (bpm); 1–10-year-olds breathe at somewhere between 24–30 bpm, 11–18-year-olds at 12–16 bpm and finally those above 18 years old 12–20 bpm – astonishing, isn't it!?

Just as puppy training takes time and effort, the more you practise slowing down your breathing, the easier it becomes. The next exercise encourages you to find your own Soothing Rhythm Breathing and involves slowing your breathing to a comfortable, deep and regular rate.

Soothing Rhythm Breathing (SRB)

This is a specific breathing practice that aims to switch on and develop an experience of feeling soothed, relaxed and calm. SRB also includes an element of mindfulness. So when you become mindful that your attention has moved away from the exercise, this is an opportunity to train your attention and gently bring it back to your breathing. You can download a recording of the exercise at https://overcoming.co.uk/715/resources-to-download.

Soothing Rhythm Breathing

1. Start by finding a place that is, as far as possible, free from distractions.

2. If you can, sit with an upright posture, feet on the floor hip-distance apart, hands gently resting on your lap. If you're listening to an audio of the exercise it's helpful to close your eyes, or you may prefer to settle your gaze gently on a fixed point (perhaps the base of a picture frame or a mark on the floor).

3. Feel strength in your spine, paired with a relaxation in your body and create a sense of openness in your chest (an open body posture).

4. Sit quietly for a moment and bring your attention to your breathing. Notice the air going in and out of your body – maybe through your nose and mouth . . . be aware of the rise and fall of your belly and your ribcage expanding then contracting.

5. As you breathe out say 'body slowing down' with a warm, caring tone of voice in your mind. Imagine your voice tone is similar to the one you use if speaking to someone you care about. Now see what it's like to alter the phrase a little – so, still with the out-breath, and with a friendly voice tone, repeat the phrase 'mind slowing down'. Notice how you feel as you do this . . . mind . . . slowing . . . down.

6. It may help to breathe in to your own count of three . . . pause and then exhale, again to a count of three . . . find a breathing pattern that, for you, seems to be your own soothing, comforting rhythm. Maybe experiment a little with your breathing . . . breathe a little faster and then a little slower and notice the difference in how your body feels.

7. Once you have found a soothing rhythm, experience it for a few minutes . . . allowing the air to come into your body slowly and evenly, and then leave it . . . slowly and evenly, in a breathing rhythm that is calming for you.

With the knowledge that you can return to this exercise at any time, gently bring the exercise to a close and widen your awareness to the chair that's supporting you and the room that you're in. If your eyes have been closed, open them: lift your gaze. Take some calming breaths and maybe have a stretch before you write about what you noticed.

How did you find the breathing practice?

REFLECT

Try to set time aside each day over the next week or so to practise SRB and 'get your body on board'. If you wish to practise for longer, or multiple times during the day, feel free to do so.

PRACTISE

TOP TIPS

- It can be difficult for any of us to engage regularly with a practice, but many people find learning to breathe calmly, smoothly and rhythmically is one of the most important things they've done and is something that's helpful to continue.

If you wanted to learn to swim, you wouldn't start by jumping in the deep end of a swimming pool or the middle of the ocean – that would be a recipe for disaster! The shallow end of a swimming pool is designed to help you practise a few strokes (ensuring you can touch the bottom, of course). The ability to swim in trickier situations comes with practice and swim fitness.

In the same way, it's helpful to train yourself in breathing practices, starting when you're already relaxed and calm. As you become more familiar and proficient with practising smooth, calm and rhythmic breathing, you'll be able to use your new breathing skills in trickier situations.

Adding method acting into the mix

Simply put, 'method acting' involves connecting with our past experiences and / or using observations of other people to portray a character. Robert De Niro (a famous method actor) allegedly got his cab driver's licence and worked as a taxi driver prior to filming *Taxi Driver* so he could get 'into the shoes' of the character he portrayed.

So, if we want to portray an angry character, it can help to bring to mind a time we've felt angry. We might also copy the body posture, movements, facial expression and breathing rate of someone who's livid! The combination of a raised chin, clenched jaw, tense muscles, rapid breathing and furrowed brow is likely to help us connect physically and emotionally with the experience.

In contrast, portraying a relaxed, calm person is going to be helped by recalling a time when we were calm. Alternatively, we would copy the 'physicality' of someone who we think looks relaxed. The combination of relaxed shoulders and facial expression, and a slow breathing rate, is likely to help us evoke a relaxed version of ourselves.

Act One   Act Two   Finale

You've already gone through a process of imagining and experimenting with your body posture, movements, facial expression and breathing rate to give you important insights. So now you're going to combine such insights with method acting. We're not wanting you to become a character in your own life; we're simply wanting you to be the version of yourself you want to be more of the time, have been in the past or want to be in the future.

Being the version (of you) you want to be

You would probably agree that it would be helpful if you were calm during interviews, confident during dates and relaxed in crowds. In this next section, you'll focus on how to use method acting principles and adjust your body posture, movements, facial expression and breathing to help you become the version (of you) you want to be.

The next worksheet asks you to consider how you would like to *be*, for example, more relaxed, confident or less anxious. You'll then use your body posture, movements, facial expression and breathing to increase the likelihood of achieving your goal. For example, if you want to work on your confidence it can help to think about a time when your body posture, movements, facial expression and breathing demonstrated confidence. You can use your own experiences as 'material' but if it helps, use your observations of other people too. The worksheet also asks you to think about times when you can practise being this 'version of you' and provides space where you can make notes and review your progress.

Before you begin, take a look at Katrina's story and her completed worksheet.

Katrina loved drama classes but regularly got stage fright. She didn't want anxiety to affect her performances so decided to 'get her body on board' by making some changes. Thinking back to times when she felt calm and relaxed, Katrina recognised she tended to walk with her shoulders down (instead of around her ears), had a 'resting' facial expression and breathed slowly. She brought to mind a friend, who had minimal nerves before performances and decided to copy her open body posture.

Katrina's Version of Me Worksheet

The version of me I'm cultivating and strengthening:

My relaxed self

Body posture and movements: Relaxed shoulders, open stance

Facial expression: Resting face

Breathing: Slow

Practise	How did it go?
Each night, at home on my own for a week	Felt a bit strange at the start of the week but I did end up feeling relaxed
When I'm walking to and from work — for a week	A bit more tricky because my mind wandered but I was able to refocus
When I'm walking to and from drama class	This was easy because I love drama
During drama class	This was relatively easy and I'm starting to become really familiar with the relaxed version of me now
Before rehearsals	I could feel my anxiety rising but I was able to make helpful adjustments to my body posture, movements, facial expressions and breathing rate and it really helped
Before my performance	I wasn't anxiety free but the body-focused tips really helped me keep my nerves in check and I gave a better performance

You can see from Katrina's example, as she progresses, she begins to practise in more difficult situations. See if you can do the same. If it helps, have a look at the Top Tips box before you make a start.

- Take your time and progress at your own pace.
- Consider what general day-to-day activities, times or locations you could use as a prompt to practise. For example, could you practise when you're on your way home from work, on your lunch break, at home, with friends or while walking your dog?

- The more you practise in relaxed or neutral situations the easier you'll find trickier situations.
- Cultivating the version of yourself you want to be takes time. Of course you will have setbacks but, just like learning to ride a bike, you can master it.

My Version of Me Worksheet

The version of me I'm cultivating and strengthening: _____ Body posture and movements: _____ Facial expression: _____ Breathing: _____	
Practise	How did it go?

You can use method acting in a range of situations and practise many different versions of yourself.

Next time you have some of that well-meaning advice we started the chapter with, or you're feeling angry, anxious or down, remember the simple mantra **Body Face Breathing**, **Body Face Breathing**, Body Face Breathing, Body Face Breathing . . . and make helpful adjustments!

My Kindness Box

Before you move on to the next chapter spend some time considering what you would like to add to your Kindness Box. Could you add photos of times you looked relaxed or calm and pictures where your body posture and facial expression were consistent with how you would like to feel in the future? How about adding a note to remind yourself to breathe slowly and calmly and to practise your Soothing Rhythm Breathing?

Summary

In this chapter, you have:

❖ Considered how your feelings naturally influence your body posture, movements, facial expression and breathing

❖ Altered your body posture, movements, facial expression and breathing to explore the impact they have on you

❖ Used 'method acting' to summon up the version of you that you want to cultivate and strengthen

❖ Considered additions to your Kindness Box

Additional notes

What will help me be kinder to myself?

What can I add to my Kindness Box?

9 Getting to know your feelings

Imagine a life without feelings. It'd be *VERY* different. It's likely there would be some feelings you would like to do without and others you would want more of, yet the simple fact is they are a very important part of our lives. So, they are here to stay but, thankfully, we can learn to understand and master them.

Feelings have an impact on the kind of day we have, our thoughts, behaviour, physical sensations and even the memories that spring to mind. Simply noticing and naming our feelings has been found to be beneficial for our wellbeing. It's also the starting point that helps us figure out:

1. Why our *bodies* respond in different ways

2. Why certain *thoughts* run through our mind

3. Why we *behave* in particular ways

As we begin to notice what triggers our 'welcome' and 'not-so-welcome' feelings we can then make changes to get them working *for* rather than *against* us.

In this chapter, you're going to:

- Focus on naming, noticing and predicting feelings
- Complete a My Feelings Worksheet
- Consider the impact mixed feelings have on you
- Explore how we learn about feelings
- Think about what to add to your Kindness Box

Naming and noticing feelings

It's amazing to recognise that we have so many different feelings that can change so quickly. We may read a negative comment on social media and feel sad, but later that day we may pass our driving test and feel joy and happiness. We all experience different feelings depending on the situations we're in. Take a look at the chart below and the Top Tips box for some ideas.

When we're under pressure or feel we're in danger, we may feel	When we've achieved something, we may feel	When we're safe and content, we may feel	When we experience loss, we may feel	If we do something we think is wrong, we may feel	When we experience disgust, we may feel
Anxious	Joyful	Calm	Sad	Ashamed	Repulsed
Fearful	Excited	Peaceful	Tearful	Guilty	Shocked
Angry	Happy	Relaxed	Lonely	Embarrassed	Revolted
Frustrated	Proud	Safe	Hopeless	Humiliated	
		Accepted			

TOP TIPS

- While some people are very aware of their different feelings, others find noticing and naming them a lot trickier. If this is the case for you, it could be because little attention was paid to feelings when you were growing up or you may have had fewer opportunities to experience certain feelings.

- It's helpful to notice and name both 'positive' and 'difficult' feelings as an important starting point for understanding how they affect your body, thoughts and behaviours. It's also helpful to learn what triggers and influences them.

- Without realising it, it's easy to minimise or ignore difficult feelings by avoiding difficult situations, drinking to excess, using recreational drugs, overeating or falling into the trap of excessive gaming, gambling or shopping.

- Feelings and thoughts can often merge into one experience. However, it can be helpful to distinguish between them via this simple rule of thumb. While *feelings* are usually described in one word (happy, afraid or angry), *thoughts* usually have a longer description. For example, 'I'm rubbish', 'They don't like me' or 'This is AMAZING!'

Researchers have found that the most powerful way to manage and change how we feel is by naming the actual feeling.

Students, all with a spider phobia, were split into four groups.

The members of each group were asked to walk towards a tarantula in a container and to try and touch it (this doesn't appeal to us!). While engaging in the task each group of students was given different instructions.

| **Group 1** was told to describe the experience of being around the tarantula and name their feelings about being near it. For example, *'I'm so scared of that huge, hairy spider'* or *'I feel anxious by being near that ugly, terrifying spider.'* | **Group 2** was given instructions that aimed to make the experience less frightening and were told not to mention their fear or disgust. People in this group would say something like, *'The spider is in a container and can't hurt me.'* | **Group 3** was told to say something irrelevant to the spider. | **Group 4** was exposed to the spider but given no instruction. |

A week later, the students were asked to get close to the tarantula once more and, if possible, touch it with their finger. The results showed that the members of Group 1 (the group that labelled their fear and got closer to the tarantula) were less afraid than the other groups. This shows how naming feelings helped the participants manage the difficult situation.

Predicting feelings

Predicting your feelings, in a range of situations, is a great way to help you consider how easy it is for you to notice and name them. Read through the different scenarios and have a go at answering the questions in the How Would You Feel If . . .? Worksheet below. There's space after each question for you to add your answers.

As mentioned in the Introduction, there might be sections and chapters you want to simply skim-read. For example, you might already be very aware of your feelings, their names and how they affect you. If this is the case, simply skim-read/lightly engage with the material because you might pick up a helpful hint or a slightly different piece of information or practice to assist you.

How Would You Feel If . . .? Worksheet

How would you feel if...?

You go to see your favourite band or watch your team win

You see someone being sick in the street

Someone you care about misses your birthday

You think you're being followed

You get a puncture in your tyre

You're late for something important

You get a promotion

Someone you really like asks you out

You don't get the job you wanted

You visit a place you've wanted to go to for ages

REFLECT

What did you notice? Was it easy or difficult to predict how you would feel in each situation?

TOP TIPS

- If you knew a friend missed your birthday because they were unwell, you might have altogether different feelings compared to them missing it because they were socialising with other friends. This is important to recognise because our feelings are often influenced by the information we have to hand.

Noticing and exploring feelings

It's amazing to notice all the different feelings we have. It's a bit like those rows of sweets in an old-fashioned sweet shop – so many to choose from and so many flavours to try (and maybe some you definitely want to avoid!). An important step towards amplifying positive feelings and minimising difficult ones involves noticing when we experience different feelings. We can do this by paying attention to them (even if it's just for one week). Just imagine you're a detective investigating the role feelings play in your daily life. Uncovering their secrets can help unlock all sorts of potential avenues that can boost wellbeing.

Noticing and exploring how you feel can help you understand:

1. *What happens in your body when you experience different feelings* (your heart rate may change, you may notice you've got sweaty palms, that your voice shakes or that you want to be sick!).

2. *How often you have that particular feeling and what it's associated with* (you may feel anger, joy, anxiety, sadness or happiness more often than other emotions). You may notice that you always feel happy when you're with your best friend but feel anger or frustration when you're with your older or younger brother or sister!

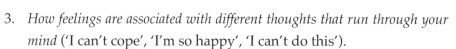

3. *How feelings are associated with different thoughts that run through your mind* ('I can't cope', 'I'm so happy', 'I can't do this').

4. *What different feelings motivate you to do* (anxiety might mean you hide away, fear might urge you to run away or avoid a situation, while happiness might mean you contact a friend and suggest doing something fun together).

Have a go at completing the My Feelings Worksheet. The first column is blank for you to add the feelings you experience over the course of a week. The second, third and fourth columns encourage you to notice what triggered the feelings, where you felt physical sensations in your body and how you reacted to the feelings. Later on in the book we'll focus on managing and expressing feelings, behaviour change and thinking traps, but for now just notice what happens when you experience the feeling and consider what the feeling motivates you to do or not do.

It might be helpful to complete an entry:

•   Whenever you notice a particular feeling

•   At the end of the day

•   On your phone

My Feelings Worksheet

My Feelings Worksheet

Anger Fear Anxiety Disgust Joy Pride Relaxed Sadness Shame Guilt Happiness

Feeling	What triggered the feeling? Who was I with?	How did my body respond? Did I notice physical sensations in my stomach, head, neck, heart and/or face?	How did I react? What did I do? Did I want to run away, hide, hit out, cry, jump for joy or phone someone?			

See what works for you. If it's not a particularly eventful week, or if it's helpful to monitor your feelings for longer, feel free to do so. Another sheet is available on page 277.

What else did you notice? Did you experience certain feelings more or less frequently than others? If it was a difficult feeling, what helped you calm down? Did you talk to someone about how you felt?

_____

_____

_____

You may have noticed in some situations that you had multiple feelings almost simultaneously. This is very common and is the focus of the next section. Let's take a closer look.

Experiencing different feelings at the same time

It's likely, at times, you'll have a mixture of feelings. For example, if you're going on a date, starting a new job, or leaving college to start university, you're likely to have mixed feelings, such as excitement, anxiety and possibly fear or sadness. This is all very understandable, but left unchecked certain feelings can dominate and result in us taking particular action (or inaction). Let's have a look at Ella's story.

Ella had tickets for a local festival and had spent the last 6 months excited to hang out with friends, and see her favourite bands. As the weekend approached, she noticed her excitement was turning to anxiety (and a little fear). She really didn't like big crowds and began questioning whether she wanted to go. As Ella pushed a sleeping bag into her rucksack, she experienced other feelings too.

Ella's situation: Going to a festival with friends

Ella has two options.

1. If she acts on the feelings of anxiety, fear and doubt, she may avoid going to the festival and could later regret her decision.

2. If Ella reminds herself that she'd felt excited and happy earlier and tells herself that experiencing a change or mixture of feelings is perfectly normal when facing something challenging, then this may help her to decide to go to the festival.

Can you think of a situation where you've experienced a mixture of feelings? Maybe you have a good example from your Feelings Worksheet. If you can recall a situation, have a go at completing your own diagram.

My situation

How did your feelings influence your behaviour? For example, did you avoid a situation due to the difficult feelings and physical sensations?

_____

_____

_____

If you felt the uncomfortable feelings but still faced the situation, what helped?

_____

_____

_____

If your feelings did influence your behaviour in a way that you were not happy with, don't worry: we'll look at how you can tackle that in the following chapters. For now, it's enough just to notice whether your feelings influenced what you did.

Formative learning about feelings

During the course of this chapter, you may have been wondering why you are the way you are or feel the way you do. Like many other areas of our lives, we learn about feelings via many routes. Parents, caregivers, role models, friends and family influence how much we notice feelings, the words we use to describe them and even how we express them. We also absorb messages from books, films, magazines, social media, lyrics and the internet and we may have even attended classes at school that focus on feelings.

 Just imagine if someone had been told as a child *'Don't be such a baby'* when they cried or felt sad, or *'Pull yourself together'* when they felt angry: what impact would that have on them? What about if they were told *'Don't get ahead of yourself'* or *'Don't count your chickens before they're hatched'* when they were excited about something? How could that impact on them?

_____

_____

_____

Experiencing those situations may make it more likely that they would grow up struggling to express how they felt or grow up thinking that it's wrong to express certain feelings.

Expressing feelings

We'll focus on managing and expressing feelings in the next chapter, but for now let's have a look at some initial ideas about *our right to express how we feel.*

Imagine you're having a party and you've invited all your friends. They've all told you they will be there. On the day, one of them simply texts to say they can't make it with no explanation. How would you feel? You may not be bothered, but if it's a close friend who's promised to be there and then cancelled you may feel angry, disappointed and/or sad, especially if you had been looking forward to spending time with them. You may even start to wonder . . .

Of course, you may be jumping to conclusions or taking it much too personally when there is a perfectly good explanation. Whether you've done so or not, if difficult feelings remain, a helpful response might be to tell your friend how you feel. The key here is that it's important to remember that you have the right to express how you feel and if you can, do so without judgement of the other person. You never know: something may have come up they couldn't avoid, or they might be terrified in large groups of people!

You might for example, say to your friend . . .

We'll explore how you can use creative ways to tone down, turn up, manage and express feelings in the next chapter, and we'll also focus on building assertiveness skills in more detail in Chapter 14.

My Kindness Box

Finally, just think about possible additions to your Kindness Box. What will remind you to spend time noticing and naming your feelings? Would it help to put a copy of your Feelings Worksheet in your Kindness Box? How about creating your own emojis and adding those? Could you add something about the benefits of experiencing different feelings – life would be poorer without them even though some are difficult to manage. Some people find quotes, lyrics or inspirational statements helpful. Here are a couple of examples:

'Stars can't shine without darkness.'

– D. H. Sidebottom

'Courage doesn't always roar. Sometimes it's the little voice at the end of the day that says I'll try again tomorrow.'

– Mary Anne Radmacher

Summary

In this chapter, you have:

❖ Focused on noticing and naming feelings

❖ Completed a Feelings Worksheet

❖ Reflected on times when you have experienced different feelings at the same time

❖ Discovered that we learn about feelings in our formative years (from role models, family, friends and the media)

❖ Considered additions to your Kindness Box

Additional notes

What will help me be kinder to myself?

What can I add to my Kindness Box?

10 Creative ideas to help you manage and express feelings

In this chapter, we're going to continue to focus on feelings because they affect our lives in *so* many ways. It's helpful not to see feelings as an immovable or unchangeable part of our lives, but as a set of experiences we have some influence over. That's not to say we're likely to feel happy before an interview or joyous when our pet is sick, but it can help to work on and work through some of the feelings we have. This might mean sitting with difficult feelings (instead of avoiding them), amplifying positive ones, toning down those that are difficult and expressing those that might otherwise eat us up. We'll explore some of the ways we can do this in this chapter.

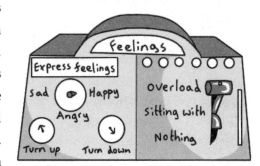

In this chapter, you're going to:

- Consider how music, art and writing can help you manage and express feelings

- Explore how focusing your attention on good things can enhance wellbeing

- Contemplate using a video diary to help you manage and express feelings

- Create a mind map with ideas about what will help you when you experience difficult feelings

- Think about what to add to your Kindness Box

Many people find it helpful to tap into their creative side in order to manage and express their feelings. Let's start by taking a look at how music can help.

Appreciating the power of music

You probably know the type of music that helps you relax, have fun, inspires or motivates you. Film makers use music to great effect, evoking a full range of feelings in the viewer to enhance scary, romantic, uplifting, dramatic and/or funny scenes. Next time you're watching a scary movie, experiment by turning the sound down for a few seconds and notice how that changes your experience of the film.

Music is often used by actors and athletes before important events. In these situations, music is used to help motivate, increase performance levels, connect with feelings or manage anxiety. You may have noticed sports personalities 'getting in the zone', wearing headphones before a match or as they walk out into a sports arena.

TOP TIPS

- Music is very personal, so bear in mind something that your friend might find soothing, inspirational, motivational, calm or fun may not be the music that soothes you or gets you up on the dance floor wanting to show off your latest moves!

You may already have a playlist for certain situations but it's also helpful to create a playlist for when you want to turn up, tone down, sit with and express different feelings. Have a look at the Music and Me Worksheet and see if you can create a playlist for different occasions. There's space at the bottom of the worksheet for you to add further ideas if that would be helpful. For example, you may want to add a playlist to help you wake up in a morning and/or one you can shout your head off to and get your frustration or anger out!

Music and Me Worksheet

Music and Me

Music that helps me when I feel sad

Music I like to listen to when I feel happy

Music that helps me when I feel anxious

Music that helps calm me when I feel angry

Music that helps inspire me

Music that helps motivate me

Music that helps me feel relaxed, soothed and calm

Music that helps me prepare for physical and psychological challenges

Music that I like to have fun and dance to

Other situations I would like a playlist or song for

TOP TIPS

- Dancing and/or singing can increase feel-good hormones and can be beneficial in helping change how we feel, reduce tension and anxiety, and there's the extra bonus of doing some exercise!

- Playing an instrument, joining a band or learning to play a piece of music can also help wellbeing. Music has been found to improve self-expression, team building, memory, social skills and help people manage anxiety.

- Even if you're not musically inclined, playing an instrument can help relieve stress and can also be enjoyable (although your loved ones or neighbours may not like it if you suddenly decide you want to learn to play the drums!).

- Music can help us to connect with other people. Listening to music with friends or checking out if your local community or sports centre has music or dance classes is a good way of connecting with others.

Expressing feelings through art

Some people find drawing, painting, photography or creating something artistic (designing bracelets, T-shirts and so on) helps them turn up, tone down, sit with and express feelings. Creating something from things that have been washed up on the beach or using leaves, sticks, sand, clay or other natural materials can also help us express how we feel. Art may help you get feelings out of your mind and body and onto paper or canvas.

TOP TIPS

- Drawing mountains to represent good experiences and valleys to represent difficult times is a creative way of expressing how you feel.

- It's common to feel overwhelmed at times, as though we're lost at sea. So how about painting, drawing or even creating a lighthouse that symbolises the guidance you need.

- Try painting to music to explore how that makes you feel.

- Try not to over-critique your artwork – it can be just for you and doesn't have to be perfect.

REFLECT

How could you use art to help you express how you feel? If you don't want to draw, paint or create something, would taking photographs help you express how you feel?

SCIENCE

Did you know that some research studies suggest that the left side of our brain is responsible for things like thinking and is our analytical, verbal and judgemental part? The right side of our brain is non-verbal and is creative and intuitive. Some researchers suggest that doing something creative, which connects both sides of the brain, helps us to manage and express feelings.

We can also turn up, tone down, sit with and express feelings through writing lyrics, music or poetry. Let's take a look.

Expressing feelings through writing

Many people write a diary or journal or do so at some point in their lives. Some people have asked us *'Why would I want to write things down, it'll only make me feel worse?'* Of course, this may be true in the short term, but long-term writing about how we feel means we're not avoiding or numbing our feelings. If you don't like writing or keeping a diary, perhaps you could try using an art journal instead.

Why writing can be helpful

1. Writing may help you get the words, anxiety and worries out of your head and onto paper.

2. Research shows that writing can be helpful and empowering because it helps people acknowledge, notice and reflect on their feelings.

3. Writing poems or lyrics may help you express how you feel.

4. Writing can play a part in the healing process.

5. Writing can help you reflect on difficulties, validate how you feel and gives you an opportunity to demonstrate kindness and understanding to yourself.

6. Writing about positive memories and the things you're grateful for can also make you feel good.

Set aside 10–15 minutes for three or four consecutive days and use this time to write freely about a single issue that's causing you anxiety or pain. Your writing doesn't have to be perfect, so don't worry about your handwriting or spelling. The aim is to just write about how you feel in a caring and kind way. Let's have a look at Tyler's story as an example.

Tyler's mum had been offered a new job, meaning the family had to move to another city. Tyler was pleased for his mum but sad for himself because he had to move away from friends and start at a new college.

Tyler acknowledged how he felt and wrote:

It's understandable that I feel sad. I don't want to move away from my friends and have to start again making new friends at a new college. I feel anxious when I meet new people... It took me ages to feel confident and comfortable with my friends and now I have to move. :(

It's then helpful to ask yourself, what would I say to a friend who was in this situation? Tyler wrote:

Is this was happening to one of my friends I would tell them that I would be sad that they were moving away too, but I would also tell them it might be exciting to have a new experience. I would also tell them that we could Facetime or phone each other. :)

Tyler still felt sad, but felt better having written about how he felt. He concluded by writing:

It's understandable that I feel sad, other people having the same experience would probably feel sad too. Mum and Dad know how I feel – it's a pain having to move but I may feel differently once I've settled in... This sadness will pass. ♥

EXPERIMENT

Is there something you would like to write about? Have a go in the space below and see how it makes you feel.

Turning up positive feelings through writing

It's easy, at the end of the day, to focus on what hasn't gone so well or focus on worrying about something in the future.

Many studies show that we naturally and automatically pay attention to things we see as threatening rather than positive. Let's look at an example.

Imagine you're going shopping for a present for a friend and you end up going into ten shops. In the first nine, the shop assistant is friendly, kind and helpful. However, when you go into the tenth shop, the assistant is rude, disinterested or ignores you. When you get home, which experience are you more likely to talk about? Although 90 per cent of your shopping experience was positive, you would probably talk about the difficult situation, because our focus naturally tends to get caught up on the negative even though this was only 10 per cent of our experience. The good news is that we can *bring balance* to our everyday experiences by focusing on the positives we've had.

It's important to remember that this negative bias in our attention and memory isn't something bad or something to criticise ourselves for. It's just helpful to remember that's the way we're made – we're more likely to pay attention to something we perceive as threatening or something that we think may be harmful to us. The good news is, once we've noticed this has happened, we can switch our attention and find balance by refocusing on positive experiences we have had.

When our attention is grabbed by the negative it can be helpful to try (just as you did in Chapter 4), to gently and kindly move the spotlight of your attention onto something you feel happy or joyful about, or that you are grateful for. We're not suggesting you ignore difficult or painful feelings: it's just helpful to find balance. One way we can do this is by writing about positive feelings and experiences.

Researchers have found that paying attention to good things (this can include things we're grateful for) can have a positive effect on wellbeing. Fancy having a go?

Three good things

For a week, write down three good things that have happened each day in the worksheet on the next page. It could be things that you've done well or something you're grateful for. If you're struggling for ideas have a look at the list of examples on page 180.

Three Good Things Worksheet

Day of the week	1st good thing	2nd good thing	3rd good thing
Sunday			
Monday			
Tuesday			
Wednesday			
Thursday			
Friday			
Saturday			

At the end of the week, having written down three good things, what do you notice?

_____

_____

_____

If you're struggling to think about three good things, here are a few examples:

- Getting positive feedback

- Receiving a nice, thoughtful text message

- Having fun with a pet

- Enjoying a walk

- Having a nice family meal

- Spending time with someone you care about

- Enjoying being outside in the sunshine or the snow

- Being treated with respect and kindness

- Having had a good night's sleep

- Receiving a compliment

- Getting through a difficult day

Using audio and video diaries to help express feelings

While famous diary writers such as Anne Frank and Nelson Mandela only had the option of putting pen to paper, we have the benefit of typing, voice recording and creating video diaries. Such technology can give us an outlet for how we're feeling, and it's a novel way of relating to ourselves.

When you're next experiencing a difficult feeling, consider capturing it in the form of a brief video diary. Speak into your phone or camera, letting the feelings and words out. Do so until you feel you're ready to stop. Then take a few calming breaths.

Having recorded the video and/or audio diary, how do you feel?

_____

_____

_____

If it helps, engage in a practice that allows you to tolerate the difficult feelings and eventually soothe them away. It may be one of your 'building block' practices from Part 2, such as a mindfulness or imagery exercise. Alternatively, you may prefer to connect using your Soothing Rhythm Breathing, or perhaps there's something in your Kindness Box that may help support you.

Now imagine, for a moment, you're sat with a friend or family member who happens to be experiencing a difficult time. Play back the audio or video diary you've recorded, listening and hearing the anxiety, anger, low mood, shock or disgust as though you're listening to someone you care about and not yourself.

With kindness, consider how you might respond to the distress you've seen and/or heard. What might you say if you were speaking to a friend or family member? What might you do?

_____

_____

_____

Finally, sit for a while and speak to yourself with kindness – offer yourself the care and support you would give to somebody you care about.

Based on the ideas covered in this chapter, those outlined elsewhere in _The Kindness Workbook_ and those you've learnt in your life so far, what helps (or could help) you turn up, tone down, sit with or express your feelings? Could/does music, writing about three good things, nature, art, talking to friends or family, writing, physical exercise or going to the top of a hill and shouting up to the sky help?

_____

_____

_____

- Sometimes going to places that make us feel good, peaceful or relaxed can help when we're experiencing difficult feelings. Could sitting in a garden, imagining your calm, peaceful place in your mind's eye, curling up in bed, going to a sports event, a family member's house or a park help?

Creating a mind map

You may have created a mind map in a previous chapter, or this might be the first you're making. The following mind map brings together ideas for when you experience difficult feelings. Have a look at Tyler's mind map and then have a go at creating your own. It might help to look back at some of the notes that you've made in the chapter.

Tyler's Mind Map: What helps me when I experience difficult feelings?

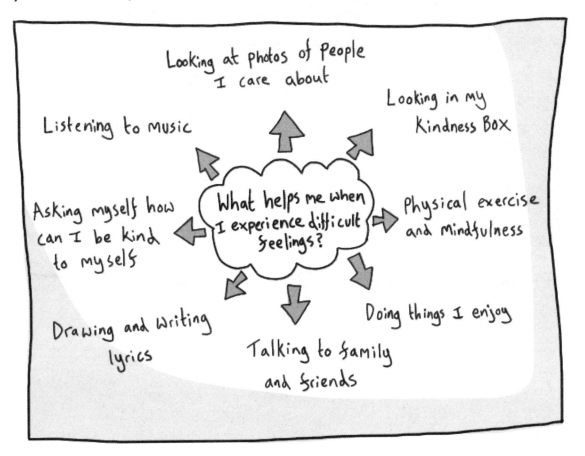

My Mind Map: What helps me when I experience difficult feelings?

My Kindness Box

So, now we're coming towards the end of the chapter, spend some time considering what you would like to add to your Kindness Box. It's not always easy to experience certain feelings, but having strategies in place that can help you manage, express and navigate them can be really useful. What would you like to add to your Kindness Box? Maybe a playlist that empowers or motivates you or one that makes you want to sing and dance? Perhaps you could include a photograph of something you've created, or draw or paint something that you can keep in your Kindness Box. Would the lyrics of a song or poem be a useful addition? Let's take a look at what Tyler put in his Kindness Box.

He included: his soothing **C**olour (yellow), **O**bject (bracelet), **S**mell (vanilla), **M**usic (a playlist for when he wanted to dance, and one for when he wanted to motivate and inspire himself), **I**mages of his relaxing place and a picture of himself with his grandma, and **C**ards that he'd been given by special people in his life. Tyler used the mnemonic C.O.S.M.I.C. to remember some of the items in his box, just in case he didn't have easy access to it.

In the next chapter, we're going to focus on how we easily get caught up in thinking traps and how our thoughts can impact on our wellbeing. But for now, take a look at the chapter summary and, if it helps, make some notes.

Summary

In this chapter, you have:

❖ Learnt that expressing how you feel is important to your wellbeing

❖ Explored how creative exercises (music, writing lyrics, painting, art, writing about how you feel and/or recording a video diary) can help you turn up, tone down, sit with and express feelings

❖ Focused on how thinking about good things can help boost wellbeing

❖ Created a mind map as a reminder of what helps you when you experience difficult feelings

❖ Considered additions to your Kindness Box

Additional notes

What will help me be kinder to myself?

What can I add to my Kindness Box?

11 Cultivating supportive thoughts

Apparently, we have between 12,000 and 70,000 thoughts each day (we haven't counted them ourselves!). We can have exciting, constructive, supportive, kind, peaceful and compassionate thoughts such as:

We can also have critical, undermining, looping or worrying thoughts, for example:

The way we think can have a **big** impact on what we **feel** and can also influence our behaviour. For example, if we have critical, worrying or undermining thoughts:

1. We may feel tense, panicky, sickly or shaky, or may notice that our heart seems to be beating faster *(physical sensations)*

2. We may *feel* sadness, fear or anger

3. We may want to run away from the situation, avoid people or hide away *(behaviours)*

Of course, if we have nice thoughts, such as, 'Wouldn't it be great if I get that job' or 'Wouldn't it be great if I won the lottery', we're likely to experience pleasant feelings (although our heart may skip a beat when we start thinking about what we'd spend the money on!).

In this chapter, you're going to:

- Notice, observe and identify different types of thoughts and thinking traps

- Complete a My Thoughts and Me Worksheet

- Compare how you speak to yourself versus how you might speak to a friend

- Develop balanced, supportive and kind thoughts

- Complete a Thought Balancing Worksheet

- Explore how coping statements can help you prepare for challenges

- Create a mind map to remind you how to deal with difficult thoughts

- Think about what to add to your Kindness Box

The way we think can make us feel anxious, angry or not good enough, but the good news is we can learn to change the way we think, which in turn can help us change the way we feel *and* behave. The first step is simply to start noticing and observing our thoughts.

Did you know?

- By the time you are twenty years old you'll have spent about 175,200 hours thinking!

- If you've spent the majority of time talking to yourself in a bullying, critical or condemning voice, changing that voice by retraining your mind will take time.

Mastering any new skill requires effort, patience and self-kindness. So, try and remember to be kind to yourself as you engage in the following six steps:

1. Noticing and observing thoughts

2. Identifying the traps you get caught up in

3. Considering the tone of voice you speak to yourself in

4. Considering if you're judging yourself harshly

5. Gaining balance

6. Getting creative!

Step 1 Noticing and observing thoughts

It's helpful first to notice the thoughts (and/or mental images) occupying your mind. Over a 24-hour period have a go at logging them using the My Thoughts and Me Worksheet.

- Thoughts often come in the form of words, for example *'I've got work tomorrow'*, *'I'm an idiot'*, *'I must book my train tickets'* (hopefully not all at the same time!). But they can also take the form of mental images such as an image of how someone *might* see you, or an image of yourself in the dentist's chair. As such, the My Thoughts and Me Worksheet prompts you to consider images too.

- You may find it easier to complete the exercise when you notice a change in feelings, physiology or behaviours.

- You could set a reminder on your phone – the notification (be it a bell, song or miaow!) can be a great way to prompt you to consider the thoughts you're having.

My Thoughts and Me Worksheet

Time of day	What thought went through your mind? Did you notice any mental images?	What physical reactions did you notice? Palpitations, sweaty palms, dry mouth, dizziness	What feelings were associated with the thought/image?	What did you do? Were there any behaviours associated with the thought? Did you try and avoid the thought or react to it?
Morning				
Afternoon				
Evening				

Did you notice any patterns, surprises or recurring themes? Did you log any supportive and kind thoughts and / or images about yourself or others?

_____

_____

_____

Don't worry if, like the majority of people, you noticed critical, undermining, looping or worrying thoughts. The following steps are designed to help.

Step 2 Identifying the traps you get caught up in

It's easy to get caught up in critical, undermining, looping or worrying thoughts. We call these 'traps' because they can get us stuck and are usually unhelpful. They fuel difficult feelings, have a negative impact on mood and ultimately decrease the likelihood that things will go well. Being aware of these thinking traps can help you get a bit of distance from your thoughts.

Have a look at the worksheet on page 192 to see which thinking traps you have a tendency to fall into. Make some notes about your own experiences.

Identifying Thinking Traps Worksheet

Thinking traps	Scenario	Can you remember a time you had a similar experience or thought?
All or nothing thinking Everything is either black or white, good or bad. There's no middle ground. For example, 'I always get it wrong' or 'I'll never get a job'.	*Reese was learning to drive but was finding a particular manoeuvre extremely difficult. Rather than think 'I can do this ... practice makes perfect,' Reese thought, 'I'm useless, I'll never pass my test, I'm rubbish.'*	
Catastrophising A tendency to overestimate danger/disaster. For example, exaggerating how bad a situation may be.	*Reuben got a low grade for a piece of coursework. 'I'm going to fail my final year,' he thought.*	
Jumping to conclusions In a way, this is like fortune telling. Without looking at facts, we jump to conclusions, assuming our conclusions are correct. For example, predicting that negative things will happen.	*Maddie didn't identify with being male or female. 'Nobody'll understand how I feel. They'll think I'm weird if I ask them to use them, they or their when referring to me,' they thought.*	
It's all my fault Sometimes this is called personalising. For example, taking responsibility for every negative experience that happens to you or other people.	*Mel's friend was really down. 'I haven't been in contact with them so much, because of exams – it's my fault,' Mel thought.*	
Labelling Giving yourself or another person a global negative label. For example, telling yourself 'You're stupid' or labelling others 'Useless'.	*Billie missed a penalty and thought, 'I'm such a loser.'*	

- Knowing the thinking traps you fall into can help you escape them!

Step 3 Considering the tone of voice you speak to yourself in

It's helpful to view thoughts as simply a way of talking to ourselves – thoughts are like the narrative to our lives. And there are two vital components to consider:

- **What** we say to ourselves (the focus of Steps 1 and 2)

- **How** we say it

Our tone of voice can change words that feel warm and encouraging to those that are undermining and hostile.

Take the phrase *'You can do this'* and, using your imagination, consider the following scenarios:

- An amazingly supportive teacher says *'You can do this'* just before an exam

- Friends cheer *'You can do this!'* as you get to the last 100m of a sponsored 5K

- Your boss shouts *'You can do this!'* as they bring an extra pile of papers to you to file

Interesting, isn't it? It's not just the things we say to ourselves that impact how we feel, but also *how* we say them.

For each of the thoughts you recorded in Steps 1 and 2, consider the tone of voice you spoke to yourself in. Was it critical, undermining, worried, excited, constructive, supportive, kind, compassionate, disgusted or angry? Did your tone of voice reflect the feeling you experienced and recorded at the time? If it helps, have a look at Bilal's story before you make some notes.

Bilal got a low assignment grade and realised he'd misread the question. 'I'm stupid,' he thought. Bilal felt really down and left college early. He later realised he'd fallen into the trap of 'labelling' himself. He also acknowledged he was speaking to himself in a really critical and undermining way. Although Bilal was still disappointed, he found such realisations really helpful.

Have you noticed if there's a particular voice tone that you tend to use when talking to yourself? When and how often do you use that voice tone?

Step 4 Considering if you're judging yourself harshly

Referring back to the thoughts you've logged, and the tone of voice you used, were you judging yourself harshly? If a friend or family member found themselves in a similar situation, would you speak to them in the same way? What might the consequences be if you spoke to them in an undermining and critical way? What words of kindness and tone of voice could you use instead?

_____

_____

_____

 Bilal wrote:

> I wouldn't tell someone I love they're stupid, and I wouldn't speak to them with the same critical and undermining tone as I speak to myself. I would be more supportive and kind – letting them know we all make mistakes and it's likely they'll learn from it and do better next time.

REFLECT

What can you learn from this? Are you speaking to yourself in the same way as you speak to others? If not, how would you like to speak to yourself?

_____

_____

_____

Bilal wrote:

> Although I was critical of myself at the time, it's great that I'm able to reflect on the situation. I'll remind myself to treat myself the same way I treat others and I'll make more of an effort to be kinder to myself.

Step 5 Gaining balance

Before we focus on Step 5 let's recap. So far, you've:

1. Spent some time noticing and observing thoughts

2. Recognised traps you get caught up in

3. Figured out that tone of voice is important

4. Considered if you're judging yourself too harshly. And if you are you've hopefully realised that you wouldn't speak to someone you cared about in this way (or a stranger for that matter!).

Step 5 involves learning to think in a more supportive, kind and balanced way rather than a critical or undermining way. Before we look at how to cultivate more balanced thoughts, have a look at the Top Tips section for examples of supportive and kind statements.

TOP TIPS

- Remind yourself that situations like this happen to other people too. Feelings and moments of anxiety are a natural part of life . . . and do change.

- Focusing on being supportive and kind is healthier and more helpful than being critical and undermining.

- Life is hard – and we all make mistakes from time to time.

- Remind yourself that thoughts are just events in your mind. You have thousands of thoughts every day – and *thoughts are not necessarily facts!*

- Trying to stand back and describe (rather than judge) the situation helps break the link between thinking something and believing it's true.

Remember to tell yourself that you're proud of yourself for trying to cultivate supportive and kind thoughts.

Cultivating balanced thoughts

Over the next week or so try to notice any critical, worrying or undermining thoughts. You may notice one thought (although they do tend to come in packs!). Alternatively, you might notice a change in physical sensations, feelings or behaviour first. If that's the case, consider the thought or image that accompanied that change.

Detecting and analysing thoughts means trying to be objective by looking at facts. So, just like a detective examines the evidence at a crime scene, you'll need to examine the evidence for and against your thoughts – so put yourself into the shoes of your favourite detective (Sherlock Holmes, perhaps) or Superhero (Black Panther or Wonder Woman)! You may prefer to use characters from your favourite book, or you may want to use your Kindness Crusader to help! Remember you need someone who'll help you cultivate supportive and kind thoughts, so you can bring balance to your mind.

When you notice or observe a thought, work through the following questions, using a supportive, kind, gentle and caring tone of voice. If you notice that you're being critical, perhaps think of someone you really care about and consider how you would help them if they were in your shoes. A kind, supportive friend wouldn't be critical, but neither would they say *'You did amazing'* if you messed up or *'Let's do something else'* if you had a dental appointment you were fearful of. A supportive friend would say *'You tried your hardest and I'll help you practise next time if you want'* or *'I'll come to the dentist with you if that would help you.'*

Examining the evidence

What were you thinking? Did any images occupy your mind?

REFLECT

_____

_____

_____

What type of thought was it? Was it a critical, worrying, undermining or looping thought? Were you caught in a thinking trap (have a look back at the earlier steps if that helps)?

_____

_____

_____

Weigh up the evidence for and against the thought. Would somebody who cares about you say your thought is/was 100 per cent fact? Would they say the evidence supports this thought?

_____

_____

_____

Is there an alternative view of this situation?

_____

_____

_____

Now you've examined the evidence, is there a more balanced thought?

_____

_____

_____

Looking at the balanced thought, if you were to hear it, what tone of voice would be helpful to use? What voice tone would you use if you were speaking to a friend?

_____

_____

_____

Having generated a balanced thought, are there any further reflections that would be worth writing down? Having looked at the facts, are you underestimating how well you dealt with the thought?

_____

_____

_____

Learning how to respond with care and kindness

If you're struggling for time and need a shorthand way to examine the evidence before you, you may like to use our four-column Thought Balancing Worksheet to identify the thought, consider the evidence supporting it, the evidence against it and then see if you can generate a more balanced and realistic view.

Remember to use a supportive and kind tone of voice.

At the start of Part 3 we introduced you to Jess. Let's have a recap and look at how she used the Thought Balancing Worksheet to examine the evidence for and against the thoughts she was having.

Jess received a text message from her best friend Cerys saying they'd been invited to a New Year's party. On receiving the invite, Jess felt a sudden wave of anxiety. 'Oh no, what if I don't know what to say to people when I get there?', 'What if I stutter or blush when I'm spoken to?', 'I want to go . . . but what if I end up on my own, looking like a spare part?'

Using her inner 'Hermione Granger' to investigate the evidence for and against her thoughts, Jess was able to generate more balanced, supportive and kind ones.

Jess's Thought Balancing Worksheet

Thought	Evidence for my thoughts	Evidence against my thoughts	A balanced view
What if I stutter or blush when spoken to?	I've blushed before, I went red at work last week when I didn't know the answer to a question	I blush sometimes but I've never stuttered	Try not to jump to conclusions Just because I blush occasionally doesn't mean I'm a bad person Everyone feels anxious at times
What if I don't know what to say to people when I get there?	Can't think of any evidence for this, but it could happen	Cerys is going and we never stop talking — I'll chat to her	I've been catastrophising Most people think I'm ok I'll focus on other people so if I do see people I know, I'll just ask them how they are
I want to go...but what if no one likes me?	Joe sometimes ignores me - that might be evidence that someone doesn't like me	I had a nice chat to Amir last week - he asked me to help him with his coursework	I've been caught up in an 'all or nothing' thinking trap, thinking everything is either black or white, good or bad

Have a go at examining your thoughts, looking for the evidence for and against them.

My Thought Balancing Worksheet

Thought	Evidence for my thoughts	Evidence against my thoughts	A balanced view

Stressful situations are a part of life and can be tricky for us all. The key is to face our fears, even though it may be difficult.

> *'Sometimes in life you don't always feel like a winner,*
> *but that doesn't mean you're not a winner.'*
>
> – Lady Gaga

Step 6 Getting creative!

Using coping statements, mind maps and inspirational quotes can also help you cultivate supportive and kind thoughts. You might choose to have an inspirational quote (like the Lady Gaga quote above) or coping statements on your phone, in a book or even written on a wrist band.

Here are some coping statements to consider:

- *It's understandable that I feel like this, but this feeling is temporary*

- *Five years from now, if I look back at the situation, will I look at it any differently?*

- *Just remember to take one step at a time*

- *I'm not the only one who finds new situations tricky*

- *We're all a work in progress*

- *The way I feel in this moment isn't pleasurable, but it isn't harmful*

- *This feeling will pass*

- *It may not be as bad as I think*

- *This is important to me; I may enjoy it if I go*

- *I'm not going to let feelings and bodily sensations rule me*

- *Remember . . . just stick to the facts*

- *Worrying about or avoiding situations doesn't help me, but facing my fears does*

If you're doing something that makes you feel anxious, angry, sad or lonely it can help to prepare your mind and body for potential challenges. So, review all the different ideas and practices you've covered in *The Kindness Workbook* to date and consider combining them with supportive, kind and balanced thoughts. For example, mindfulness might help you notice the thoughts that pop up when you're trying to focus and Soothing Rhythm Breathing might help you slow down, whereas imagining your Kindness Crusader may help you be kinder to yourself. It might also help, at times, to move the spotlight of your attention to something else.

Some people like to get thoughts out of their head and onto paper. Creating a mind map is a useful way of doing this and can act as a reminder of the strategies you can use when you find yourself caught up in a thinking trap. Have a look at Jess's Mind Map before you have a go at creating your own.

Jess's Mind Map: How to deal with negative thoughts

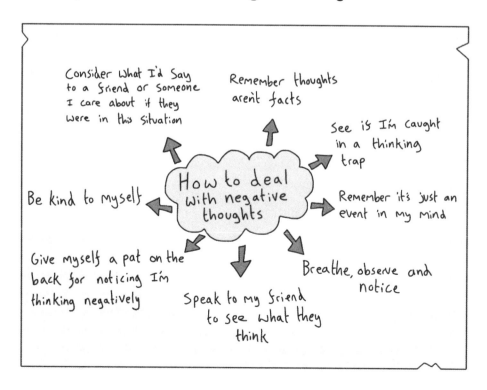

My Mind Map: How to deal with negative thoughts

We've covered quite a lot in this chapter and we hope you can see the benefits of noticing, observing and generating more balanced thoughts. The key is to respond to your thoughts with kindness using a supportive voice tone.

My Kindness Box

Before you look at the chapter summary, consider what you would like to add to your Kindness Box. Would you like to add a couple of coping statements, a mind map, the mantra *'Thoughts aren't facts'* or some notes about the thinking traps you get caught up in?

Summary

In this chapter, you have:

❖ Noticed and identified different types of thoughts

❖ Completed a My Thoughts and Me Worksheet

❖ Focused on thinking traps and how to get out of them

❖ Considered how you would speak to someone you cared about who had similar thoughts

❖ Learnt how to develop supportive, kind and balanced thoughts and completed a Thought Balancing Worksheet

❖ Explored how coping statements can help you prepare for challenges

❖ Created a mind map to act as a reminder of how to deal with tricky thoughts

❖ Considered additions to your Kindness Box

Additional notes

What will help me be kinder to myself?

What can I add to my Kindness Box?

12 Preparing for change

Have you ever noticed how your feelings and thoughts influence both what you do AND don't do? When we're *happy*, we might sing out loud, dance round the room or shrug off the worries (that kept us awake the previous night!). If we're *sad* or down, we might not feel like doing anything, may struggle to concentrate or find it difficult to do the things we usually find interesting and enjoyable. If we're *frustrated*, we might bite someone's head off, clench our fists, bite our cheek or kick a ball so hard it bounces off a (thankfully safety glass) window. Then there's *anxiety*. Anxiety can mean we avoid situations, or maybe endure them with a 'back-up' plan, such as finding out in advance where the loos are! We may notice thoughts such as 'I'll only be safe going to town with a friend' or 'If I keep my head down no one'll ask me a question'. As you can see from the examples, the way we think and feel can have a big impact on what we do *and* don't do.

In this chapter, you're going to:

- Consider if you use avoidance strategies
- Identify a change you want to make
- Explore the pros and cons of change
- Create a ladder of goals
- Imagine the changes you are aiming to make
- Create a vision board
- Think about what to add to your Kindness Box

You may have a good idea of the changes you want to make and be raring to get started. But let's first consider what can get in the way of behaviour change by focusing on something very common that we all practise at times: **avoidance**.

The power of avoidance

It's definitely a good idea to avoid:

- Swimming in shark-infested waters

- Someone who makes you feel bad about yourself

- Picking up an unexploded firework

But avoiding situations when you're *not* in danger can actually make things worse, even if it makes you feel better in the short term.

Let's consider a few examples. If we're anxious around dogs, we might avoid going to the house of a friend who has two massive canines! Short-term reduction in anxiety might be great but could have a negative impact on your friendship. Similarly, if we fear speaking in front of others, we may avoid doing a presentation. This might be great on the day, but missing the opportunity to develop presentation skills might affect job opportunities in the future (as interviews often involve speaking to a group or even standing up and giving a presentation). If we fear social situations, we might avoid them. At home, left to our own devices, we're more likely to fill our time with worry and undermining thoughts. This *supercharges our fear* for the next social situation on the horizon.

So, if we discover our behaviours are unhelpful (in the short or long term) it's useful to consider replacing them with new ones. And when we discover *helpful* behaviours, it's important to keep doing them until they become easier and more familiar – like wearing in a pair of new shoes!

One step at a time

Thankfully, we can build up our confidence, face our fears and boost well-being by focusing on behaviour change. The best way to do this is gradually. For example, if you want to improve your mood, it's helpful to start to reintroduce gradually some of the activities you used to enjoy. If you have a phobia of spiders (*arachnophobia*), clowns (*coulrophobia*), of being without your phone *(nomophobia)* or of long words *(hippopotomonstrosesquippedaliophobia* – whoever made that one up was cruel!), it would help to face your fear one step at a time. Equally, if you struggle in social situations (social phobia), your first step might be to call into your local shop to buy a loaf of bread. The next could be asking the shopkeeper a question. Future steps may include a visit to a friend's house, then going to the cinema with a friend – and then the final challenge might be going to a party.

Albert Ellis was one of the founders of Cognitive Therapy (a type of psychotherapy that looks at the way our thoughts influence us) and believed that if you do what you're afraid of doing, you'll get over your phobia. Apparently Albert knew first-hand what it felt like to have fears, because as a young man he was afraid of public speaking (he also had a fear of approaching women).

To face his fears, he forced himself to speak in public rather than avoid it. At nineteen years of age, he set himself a goal of going to the Bronx Botanical Gardens to talk to women for one minute at a time. Albert forced himself to make conversations with more than one hundred women and joked that he even managed to secure a date! She didn't show up, but he said it was a valuable lesson *'that self-confidence rarely comes from doing nothing'*. This is called exposure therapy (when you face the things you fear). If you do the thing you're afraid of often enough you'll get over your fear of it. Albert apparently faced his fear every day for a month and eventually his anxiety reduced.

Being scared of things or situations, and then avoiding them, developed out of a fundamental need to survive. For example, our ancestors may have lived somewhere that had deadly spiders or snakes, which meant they needed to be alert to danger (ready to escape to safety). Although some fears seem rational, others, at first glance, seem mind-bogglingly irrational. For example, there's no chance of us encountering a sabre-toothed tiger, yet some people still have an overwhelming fear of them and will avoid watching films or reading books in which they might appear. In such cases it's often not the sabre-toothed tiger that's the issue – it's the fear of the fear itself.

Let's have a look at how you can prepare for change by following four steps:

1. Identifying a change you want to make

2. Building an appetite for change

3. Creating a list of goals

4. Preparing your mind and body using imagery

Step 1 Identifying a change you want to make

The first step is to consider what changes would be helpful for you to make. You may want to face a fear, find a job, build confidence, be in a committed relationship, get a promotion, become more assertive, exercise, reconnect with family, change your diet or face something you've been avoiding. If you're struggling to identify a change how about flicking back to the physical health chapters (7 and 8) to see if you can find any inspiration there. Alternatively, would it be helpful to focus on something that's consistent with your values (Chapter 3) and put them into action? Let's take a look at Chloe's story and then consider if there's a change (big or small) that you would like to make.

Chloe wanted to go travelling with friends. The only problem was that she had a needle phobia and some of the countries they wanted to visit required vaccinations. Chloe wanted to overcome her phobia so she could travel safely around the world.

What change(s) would you like to make?

_____

_____

_____

Step 2 Building an appetite for change

Before you decide to make a change, it can be helpful to think about the pros (positives) of change and cons (negatives/drawbacks) of not making the change. Have a look at Chloe's Pros and Cons of Change Worksheet and then have a go at completing your own.

Chloe placed two headings on the top of a piece of paper: *'What will be the benefits of having my vaccinations?'* and *'What will be the drawbacks if I don't have my vaccinations?'*

Chloe's Pros and Cons of Change Worksheet

Pros	Cons
What will be the benefits of having my vaccinations?	What will be the drawbacks if I don't have my vaccinations?
I'll be able to go away with my friends I'll get to see places that I have dreamt of visiting I'll have quality time with my friends I'll have time to relax and have fun	I won't be able to go away with my friends I'll miss out because I won't be with them I won't get to see the places I've always dreamed of

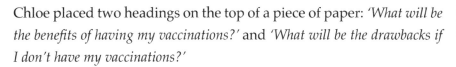

Building your appetite for change

Now it's your turn. In the left-hand column create a list of the pros of change, and in the right-hand column create a list of the cons or drawbacks of not making the change.

My Pros and Cons of Change Worksheet

Pros What will be the benefits of _____	Cons What will be the drawbacks if I don't _____

The thought of overcoming the needle phobia (and being able to travel with friends) was enough to spur Chloe on. She made the decision to learn to tolerate, master and overcome her fear.

Assuming you want to continue your journey towards change, let's take a step further by creating a list of goals. Once again, we'll use Chloe's story as an example.

Step 3 Creating a list of goals

Your list of goals could include the fears you want to face, one step at a time, or it could be a list of challenges to help you improve your mood, motivation levels, confidence or general wellbeing (for example, you may want to eat healthier, socialise more or do more exercise).

Chloe created a list of fear-inducing situations that might pave the way to her tolerating her vaccinations (after all no one's going to like them, are they?). Chloe put them in order from the most fear-inducing to the least. At the bottom of her list were the situations that she thought would be easier to face and at the top was the situation she feared the most (getting the vaccination). Have a look at the Top Tips box and Chloe's list of fears and then have a go at creating your own list.

TOP TIPS

- The first time you face something challenging, you're likely to feel an increase in anxiety. However, by staying in the situation for long enough you'll notice your anxiety reduces.

- Although changing a behaviour can be difficult, it's worth the effort in the long term – could thinking about what you want for your 'Future Self' help you?

- It can be helpful to rate the distress you feel by giving each task a score between 0 and 10. A score of 0 represents no anxiety, distress or fear and a score of 10 represents the highest anxiety you feel.

- You may prefer to include emojis that represent how you feel.

REMEMBER

Although we're using Chloe's fear and potential avoidance as an example, the process would be exactly the same if she was setting herself the goal of improving her health and fitness. For example, her goals could include: having five portions of fruit and vegetables per day; buying a gym kit; putting trainers by the side of the door; registering for a park run; or going out for a walk five times a week, before potentially building up to a park run.

Chloe's Ladder of Goals

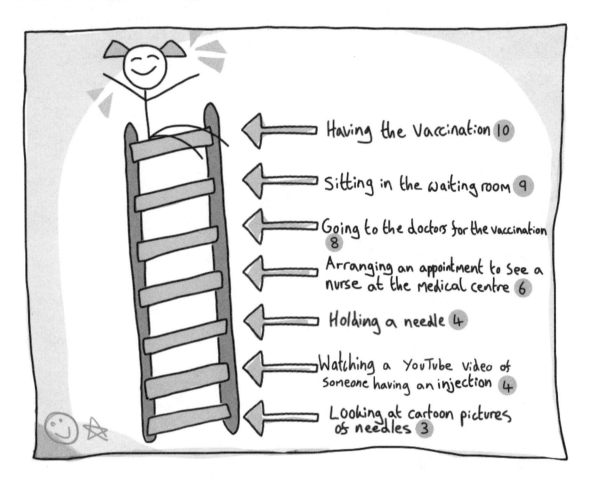

My Ladder of Goals

 Remember to put the easiest goal at the bottom of the ladder and the most difficult at the top.

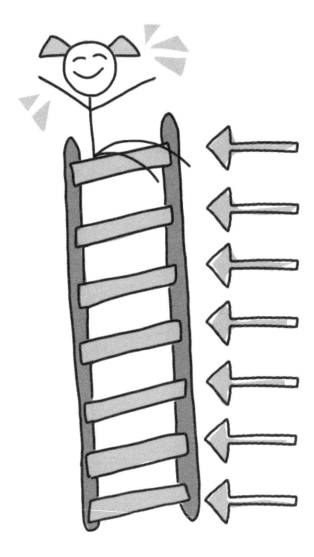

Here are three examples, focusing on different scenarios, which may give you some ideas about the goals you want to add to your list.

Social Anxiety

If you experience anxiety in social situations your list may include:

Making eye contact and saying hello to someone, asking someone how their day has been, asking a question at work, trying out for a sports team, inviting a friend to your house for a meal, ringing a company up to ask if they're looking for staff, attending a party.

Low Mood

If you experience a dip in mood and have been avoiding friends and not going to the gym your list may include:

Sending a text to one of your friends to ask how they are, going for a 10-minute walk, inviting a friend over for a chat, going to the cinema with a friend, asking someone to go to the gym with you.

Animal Phobia

If you have a fear of a specific animal your list may include:

Looking at a cartoon character of the animal you fear, looking at pictures of the animal you fear, listening to the sound the animal makes or a clip on YouTube, watching the animal from inside the house, going to the zoo or pet shop to see the animal, watching the animal while outside (for example, watching a dog on a lead, or a bird in a cage), touching the animal.

The changes you want to make may be big or small. Some of the steps on your ladder might require little preparation or imagination. You may be chomping at the bit to get your trainers out if you're planning on improving your physical fitness or you might be excited to look at different local community groups if you're planning on joining one. The reward you might get from achieving a step, and putting a *big tick* at the side of your ladder, might be all the motivation you need to move on to the next step, and the next . . . Bigger steps can be made easier by listening to music, focusing on a confident body posture and facial expression. Soothing and calming exercises, the generation of balanced thoughts and a supportive voice tone can also help.

When behaviour changes are associated with apathy or significant levels of anxiety you may find yourself doing everything (ironing, playing computer games, cleaning the bin or sorting your sock drawer!) to avoid taking that step. In such cases it can be helpful to use the power of your imagination to assist you and develop a game plan. So, the next section focuses on imagining the change you're aiming for.

Step 4 Preparing your mind and body using imagery

Let's start by using the power of imagination. This involves thinking about each situation on your ladder (one at a time), beginning with the easiest challenge (bottom rung).

Chloe decided to start by imagining she was looking at pictures of needles as this was the challenge listed on the bottom rung of her ladder.

Imagining each situation on my list

1. Once you've found somewhere to sit, gently bring your attention to your breathing, becoming mindful of it. You may choose to close your eyes or, if you prefer, keep them open and focus your gaze on the base of a picture frame or a mark on the floor. Notice the sensations as you breathe slowly in and then slowly out. It might be helpful to engage in your Soothing Rhythm Breathing (see Chapter 8). Feel your body begin to relax as you breathe slightly slower and deeper than usual. Let your shoulders drop a little and your jaw loosen.

2. You may want to imagine that your Kindness Crusader, Cheerleader, Coach, Supportive Friend, Superhero and/or Compassionate Companion is by your side helping you engage with the challenge.

3. When you're ready, create an image of yourself successfully engaging with the challenge on your list. Be mindful of your confident body posture, movements, facial expression and breathing.

4. Consider what kind and supportive things you might say to yourself. Remind yourself that you're being courageous in taking this step.

5. Remind yourself that with practice it will get easier.

6. At the end of the challenge, imagine that you see yourself smiling and pleased with your achievement. Perhaps you can imagine putting a big tick or smiley face next to the challenge you've faced on your ladder.

When you're ready, gently bring the exercise to a close and widen your awareness to the chair that's supporting you and the room that you're in. If your eyes have been closed, open them: lift your gaze. Take some calming breaths and maybe have a stretch before you write about what you noticed.

How did it feel picturing yourself achieving your goal in your 'mind's eye'? Were there any difficulties? Did you remember to be kind to yourself? What helped you?

- You may find it helpful to focus on one challenge per day or week – so don't put pressure on yourself (go at your own pace).

Creating a vision board

We discussed vision boards in Chapter 7. They're creative boards that people make to help them visualise their future. They can focus our mind on behaviour change and also serve as a reminder of what we can do to make change more likely. Let's take a look at the vision board Chloe created.

Chloe was determined to achieve her goal and have the vaccinations she needed. She created a vision board, which included helpful statements, pictures of the destinations she wanted to travel to and photos of the friends she would be travelling with.

What do I need?

All you need is your list of goals (each step on your ladder), paper, card or canvas, pens, crayons or paints. If you don't like to draw or paint, use photographs or cut out pictures from magazines. You may wish to place a photo of yourself in the middle of your board and surround yourself with images.

> • It can be helpful to look at your board every day as a reminder of what you want for yourself in the future.

My Kindness Box

Well done on working through this chapter. In Chapter 13 we're going to focus on how we can boost the probability of success, but before you move on is there anything you would like to add to your Kindness Box to inspire and help you be kinder to yourself? For example, would you like to add your vision board (or a photo of it), your pros and cons of change chart, your ladder of goals, notes with helpful statements on, or a copy of the imagery exercise so that you can use it before you face each challenge on your ladder?

Summary

In this chapter, you have:

❖ Considered the impact avoidance has on wellbeing

❖ Built an appetite for change

❖ Explored the pros of change and the cons of no change

❖ Created a list of goals on your ladder of change

❖ Used imagery to help you engage with the challenges you want to face

❖ Created a vision board

❖ Considered additions to your Kindness Box

Additional notes

What will help me be kinder to myself?

What can I add to my Kindness Box?

13 Boosting the probability of success

As we learnt in Chapter 12, improving our wellbeing usually involves making changes. Sometimes we might make big changes, but it's worth bearing in mind that small changes can make a big difference too!

Small, subtle changes (such as using a supportive and kind voice tone when speaking to yourself) are difficult or even impossible for others to see. However, they can have a *huge* impact on wellbeing. Other changes are much more noticeable and may involve facing fears, challenging anxiety or setting goals that encourage us to become more active.

So, having worked through the previous chapter and identified the changes you hope to make, it's now time to focus on strategies that remind you to be kinder to yourself and that can boost the probability of success.

In this chapter, you're going to:

- Boost the probability of success by preparing your mind and body
- Create a Pre, During and After Plan to help you manage each challenge on your list
- Think about what to add to your Kindness Box

Before we start, take another look at the ladder you created in Chapter 12 (and also Chloe's ladder).

- Don't forget the easiest challenge is always at the bottom of the ladder

- Whether you're aiming to overcome a fear or you're working towards becoming more active or assertive, change takes time

- We're all different and we're all a 'work in progress' too! If you're reading these words you definitely have something in common with a lot of other people: a motivation to make improvements to your life

- Use your supportive and kind voice tone as you focus on each goal on your list

Increasing the probability of success

Before you move on to face your challenges, it's important to recognise that things don't always go to plan! So, to increase the probability of success have a look at the 'Would it help if I . . .' table for some useful pointers.

Would it help if I . . .

- Have someone with me that will support me when I attempt a goal?

- Take something with me that calms me down and/ or reminds me I'm being brave and courageous?

- Explore the evidence for and against my thoughts (Chapter 11) to help me generate balanced thoughts as an antidote to my worries?

- Watch someone else doing what I find difficult first?

- Call on my Kindness Crusader, Cheerleader, Coach, Supportive Friend, Superhero and/or Compassionate Companion to help support me before I take each challenge?

- Use some of the coping statements I focused on in Chapter 11: for example, *'I can get through this'* or *'I'm not a prisoner of this fear any longer'*?

- Take a photo of my vision board with me to look at if I need to?

What strategies have you found helpful as you've been working through *The Kindness Workbook*? Could you use them as you face the challenges on your ladder? Let's have a look at a few options:

Music and movement

Listening to music can help focus your mind and 'get your body on board'. So if you want to feel calm you might listen to relaxing music. And if you wanted to feel strong and courageous, you could choose a song that has lyrics about those qualities or a melody that energises you.

Many famous sports personalities use music to inspire and motivate themselves before they prepare for an event. For example, Serena Williams listens to music as she's walking onto the tennis court, and the New Zealand rugby team chant and move to *The Haka* (a ceremonial dance or challenge) as they believe it gives them strength because it helps them embody the spirits of their ancestors.

REFLECT

What pieces of music or songs might help you? For example, if you're planning on facing a challenge is there a song that energises and/or empowers you? Is there a song that helps when you're feeling scared or one that you associate with kindness if you're being critical? If one of your goals is to relax more, is there a song that makes you feel calm? Maybe you could download these tracks so that you have a soundtrack to help you prepare for each step on your ladder.

_____

_____

_____

Affirmations

Throughout *The Kindness Workbook*, we've encouraged you to be supportive and kind to yourself. Exactly HOW you do this depends on the situation you find yourself in. For example, if you feel anxious it may help to spend time reassuring yourself, and if you lack motivation it may help to give yourself words of encouragement. Self-affirmations are a focused way of doing this and involve the development of catchy statements that can be used to help you *before*, *during* and *after* you tackle challenges. They start with 'I' and you say them to yourself, out loud or in your head, over and over. It can help to write them down, put them on sticky notes and/or repeat them to your reflection in a mirror. Here are some to read through for inspiration:

- *I can cope*

- *I can stand it – the more I tolerate the anxiety, the stronger I get*

- *I can do this*

- *I'm working on myself*

- *I have ups and downs*

- *I can face this*

- *I can be kinder to myself*

- *I'm considerate*

- *I'm a unique person*

- *I believe in me*

- *I'm willing to invest my time in me*

Remember to use your supportive and kind voice tone, friendly facial expression and confident body posture as you say the affirmations.

- If you want to improve your confidence, your mood, boost your general wellbeing or manage your anxiety it's really important to change your behaviour, but you're much more likely to achieve your goals with encouragement. So get your Kindness Crusader, Cheerleader, Coach, Supportive Friend, Superhero and/or Compassionate Companion on the case!

- *How you talk to yourself* is incredibly important, so watch out for any thinking traps, self-criticism or harsh vocal tones and make a conscious effort to be kind to yourself.

Focus on the part of you that you want to nurture and motivate

Remember the story of The Two Wolves in the Introduction (page 4), where a grandfather told his grandchildren that we all have two wolves inside us that represent our internal battles? As you're reading through this chapter, and if there is something you want to change, remember to feed the compassionate, joyful, generous, kind and hopeful you! Being kind to yourself, rather than critical, will help you make the change you want to see.

Exercises for the mind and body

Have a look at the exercises in the table below that aim to help prepare your mind and body. Are there any that you could use *before*, *during* or *after* each challenge to boost the probability of success?

Exercises that can boost the probability of your success	
Attention	**In Chapter 4,** you focused on how to helpfully move the spotlight of attention – 'what you focus on expands'
Mindfulness	**In Chapter 5,** you mindfully focused on your breath and the sounds around you. You also learnt that you can use mindfulness skills in your everyday life

Imagining a Calming, Peaceful, Relaxing or Soothing Place	**In Chapter 6,** you created an image of a calming, peaceful, relaxing or soothing place, which was a place that helps you feel calm, peaceful and safe
Imagining Colour	**In Chapter 6,** you focused on imagining different colours, which aim to soothe, calm or re-energise
Kindness Crusader, Cheerleader, Coach, Supportive Friend, Superhero and/or Compassionate Companion	**In Chapter 6,** you created an image of something or someone that supports you, doesn't judge you and that has your best interests at heart
Progressive Muscle Relaxation (PMR)	**In Chapter 7,** you used this exercise to help you notice the difference between your tense and relaxed state
Soothing Rhythm Breathing (SRB)	**In Chapter 8,** you used the SRB exercise to help you feel soothed, relaxed and calm

- The great thing is, you can use the skills you have learnt from *The Kindness Workbook* before, during and after you take a step on your ladder of behaviours. They can take the edge off anxiety, slow down your racing mind, boost your mood and make you feel more in control.

Is there anything you could revisit that would be helpful or would remind you to be kinder to yourself? What additional resources could you use?

Pre, During and After Plans are a great way to draw together the ideas you've generated so far, making it more likely you'll achieve your goals. Let's take a closer look.

Creating a Pre, During and After Plan

Pre, During and After (PDA) Plans (not to be confused with Public Displays of Affection!) are often referred to as 'game plans' by athletes who are particularly practised in them. Let's consider what their PDA might involve.

1. *Preparation before the event.* An athlete will prepare their body by eating certain types of food, weight training and practising particular techniques. For example, footballers spend hours after training taking penalties and free kicks. To prepare their mind they may listen to inspirational music, take part in warm-up exercises, imagine success, visualise the potential obstacles they may face and overcome, and use relaxation techniques.

2. *What will be helpful during the event?* An athlete may imagine their own 'coach' or 'cheer-leader' by their side, offering them strength and courage during the event. They may practise mindfulness: on realising their mind has wandered they will return their focus

to the current situation and on what they could do, as well as on game plan options. They use their body posture, movements and facial expression to help them 'get in the zone'. If they're in a tournament and have a break they may practise their Soothing Rhythm Breathing to help calm both mind and body.

3. *After the event.* Athletes usually do 'warm-down' exercises to minimise the risk of injury. They might have an ice bath and later in the day spend time analysing their perform-ance. They do this by looking at what went well and what didn't go so well on the day.

Before you develop your own PDA Plan take a look at Yuan's story and his Plan.

Yuan really wanted to get over his fear about speaking publicly. He decided to create a PDA plan to help him prepare for a presentation he was due to give at work. He'd worked his way up to this point by identifying and successfully achieving a whole host of other steps (preparing and then practising the presentation in front of the mirror and then rehearsing in front of family and friends). The presentation itself was at the very top!

Yuan's Pre, During and After Plan

The challenge: Speaking Publicly

Pre the challenge	During the challenge	After the challenge
Prepare the presentation	Remind myself I can tolerate anxiety and I just need to take one step at a time	Remember to praise myself
Practise in front of the mirror and then in front of my friends	Use my Kindness Crusader to give me inner support	Tell myself that I'm trying hard to cope with the anxiety I feel
Use a relaxation exercise and/or imagine my calm and peaceful place	Use the Soothing Rhythm Breathing exercise to help me slow my breathing down	Tell myself that by facing my fears anxiety gets easier to handle
Pick out something to wear which I feel comfortable in	Remind myself that thoughts are not facts, and I'm doing the best I can right now	Tell myself that facing fears is a courageous thing to do
Remind myself that facing this challenge will help me build up my confidence	Be mindful of my posture and facial expression	Write down what helped me and add things to the plan that may help me in the future
Be kind to myself - treat myself the way I would treat someone I like and care about		

My Pre, During and After Plan

The challenge:		
Pre the challenge	During the challenge	After the challenge

It can also be helpful to include a prompt on your PDA Plan – something that reminds you to give yourself a pat on the back (no matter how something has gone). Alternatively, you could add notes in the reflection section below. Have a look at Yuan's reflections as they might give you some ideas.

REFLECT

What did I learn about myself while facing the challenge?

_____

_____

_____

Yuan wrote:

I was anxious and nervous, but people didn't laugh at me, which I thought would happen. The feelings of anxiety reduced after about 10 minutes and overall, I did a good job. Preparing for the challenge was helpful and the breathing exercises did help me slow down. I felt good afterwards and I am proud of myself.

You may find it helps to repeat each challenge until you feel more confident and secure in the new skills you've developed. Remember to face each situation one at a time until you reach the top of your ladder!

My Kindness Box

Before you move on to the next chapter take some time to reflect on what you could add to your Kindness Box. Would adding your PDA Plan be helpful? Perhaps you could add a photograph, which reminds you of a fear you have faced or challenge you have mastered? Would adding the ladder (with ticks next to the steps) be a helpful reminder that you've bravely faced some of the things you've found difficult in the past?

Summary

In this chapter, you have:

❖ Considered how you can boost the probability of success

❖ Created a Pre, During and After Plan

❖ Spent time reflecting on how things went after the event

❖ Considered additions to your Kindness Box

Additional notes

What will help me be kinder to myself?

What can I add to my Kindness Box?

14 The art of assertiveness

Have you ever said something you wish you hadn't, or bitten your tongue (to stop you from saying something you wanted to) and regretted it? Assertiveness skills can help decrease the chances of this happening, giving your confidence and wellbeing a boost at the same time.

Assertiveness skills combine a whole range of elements covered in *The Kindness Workbook*, so it's a great topic for our penultimate chapter. We hope you'll discover assertiveness is an amazing *act of kindness* for you – and others too.

In this chapter, you're going to:

- Consider what assertiveness is

- Focus on 'your right to express yourself'

- Take steps towards being more assertive and confident

- Consider your own and other people's perspective

- Create an assertive formula

- Create a Pre, During and After Plan

- Think about what to add to your Kindness Box

What is assertiveness?

Assertiveness is the skill of expressing ourselves, in a non-apologetic or aggressive way, while at the same time being respectful of other people. It's good for us because it allows us to be true to ourselves. It's also good for other people because it increases the likelihood of resolving the difficulties we, and they, might have.

Distinguishing between passive, aggressive and assertive behaviour

Let's have a look at some of the differences between passive, aggressive and assertive behaviour.

	Passive	Aggressive	Assertive
Language	Hesitant and apologetic language *'I'm terribly sorry to bother you'* *'If it wouldn't be too much trouble'* Saying nothing at all!	*'The correct view is...'* *'Haven't you finished yet?'* *'You'd better...'* *'If you don't I'll...'* *'Don't be stupid'*	'I' statements *('I like', 'I think', 'I feel')* *'Can we discuss this?'* *'My experience is different'* *'How can we get around this problem?'*
Facial expression	Lip biting Jaw trembling	Scowling and sneering	Relaxed and open Neutral Curious
Voice tone	Quiet Fearful	Sarcastic, cold, harsh, loud and sharp	Firm, relaxed and warm Steady pace, sincere and clear
Body language	Hand wringing Arms crossed Hunched posture	Finger pointing or clenching fists Intruding into someone's personal space Intimidating posture – leaning forward	Open body posture
Eye contact	Looking down Avoiding eye contact	Staring and trying to intimidate	Firm eye contact – not staring

Let's think about different ways in which you might react to, and deal with, a specific situation.

Imagine you're at the cinema and the people behind you are chatting and giggling. Which behaviour would be characteristic for you?

1. I'd say nothing and try to focus my attention on the film (passive response)

2. I'd turn around and say, *'WILL YOU SHUT UP!'* (angry response)

3. I'd turn around calmly and say, *'Excuse me – can you be quiet please, I can't focus on the film while you're talking?'* (assertive response)

4. I'd have a quiet word with the cinema attendant and say, *'I'm frustrated because the people behind me are talking and giggling, I wonder if you can just listen out and ask them to be quiet if they continue?'* (assertive response)

Let's consider the options.

There will be pros and cons with each scenario. For example, if you say nothing you'll avoid potential conflict but might not be able to enjoy the film and may feel frustrated. If you respond with anger, you might think *'Well at least I stood up for myself'*, but the people behind you may talk louder or kick your chair, making things worse. If your response is assertive the positive would be that you've stood up for yourself and they might stop talking, but in the short term you might feel anxious.

Letting go of the outcome

Of course, it would be great if we could control how others react to what we say or do but it's impossible to always get the outcome we hope for. However, it can be empowering to be true to ourselves and employ assertiveness skills that increase the likelihood of a positive outcome.

How does assertiveness relate to confidence?

In short, confidence means feeling secure in ourselves and our abilities. No one person is likely to feel confident in every situation, however. For example, we might feel confident at home or playing tennis, but less so in work or in the deep end of a swimming pool! Assertiveness skills can help us navigate social situations and as a consequence,

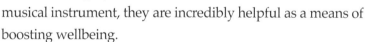

develop confidence. So although they're unlikely to help you ride a bike or play a

musical instrument, they are incredibly helpful as a means of boosting wellbeing.

Our right to express ourselves

In Chapter 9 we introduced the idea that we have the right to express how we feel and have the right to be treated with respect. Assertiveness broadens this out further and involves expressing our thoughts and opinions as well as our feelings.

In 1975, Manuel J. Smith published a book titled *When I Say No, I Feel Guilty*, introducing the idea that we all have the right to express how we feel as long as we don't disrespect the rights of other people.

This suggests that such ideas have – thankfully – been round for a long time; however, many of us still question our rights. This may be because we grew up in an environment where our rights were ignored or disrespected. Maybe we were told that expressing ourselves was selfish or disruptive to relationships. Take a look at some examples that focus on our rights of expression.

Rights of expression

- We have the right to say yes or no

- We have the right to express how we feel

- We have the right to change our mind

- We have the right to be treated with respect

- We have the right to respectfully disagree with somebody else's view

- We have the right to treat ourselves with kindness and compassion

- We have the right to say I don't know or don't understand

- We have the right to feel good about ourselves

REFLECT

Do you struggle with any of the above? If so make a few notes in the space provided.

Let's take a look at some examples where assertiveness can be difficult. Do you:

- Get tongue-tied or get into an argument if you're trying to raise something that's been on your mind?

- Find it easy to say you don't understand?

- Struggle to raise the subject if someone has upset you?

- Find it easy to express a different opinion?

Can you identify with any of the examples? Maybe some are not an issue at home but might be at work or with friends. If you *can* identify with the examples, the following section will help you learn to express yourself in an assertive way. It focuses your efforts on a situation or relationship you want to work on and improve. Once you've practised the skills, and are feeling more confident, you may find you assert yourself in much wider situations. For example, assertiveness helps when your right to return an item is questioned, or you want to express a difference of opinion in a group.

Becoming more assertive in six steps

Let's spend some time focusing on a social situation or relationship that's tricky for you. It may be one that's associated with some difficult physical sensations, feelings, thoughts and behaviours.

Mastering any new skill requires effort and patience. So try to remember to be kind to yourself as you engage in the following six steps!

1. Identifying a social situation or relationship you want to work on (for example, one where you might feel disregarded, hurt, angry or disappointed)

2. Considering your own perspective with kindness

3. Considering other people's perspectives

4. Creating an assertive formula

5. Hatching a Pre, During and After Plan

6. Reviewing progress and considering further ways forward

Step 1 Identifying a social situation or relationship that you want to work on

Some interactions are a one-off and some relationships are (thankfully) in the past. However, others might benefit from some work! See if you can identify a social situation or relationship you find tricky. Maybe you feel resentful, anxious or not able to be yourself with someone. You might be aware you're having problems  communicating your feelings, needs or viewpoint. If it's a tricky situation maybe you've not spoken up, got tongue-tied, said something you think is really lame or even spoken out a bit too much.

Take a look at the Top Tips box and Nina's story before you decide what you want to work on.

- Resist the temptation to start with the situation or person that's the most problematic for you (even though that's the one you definitely need to change!). Instead, pick a situation that's less tricky so you can build your confidence and assertiveness.

- Considering other people's perspectives doesn't mean excusing their actions or neglecting your own needs. It's simply a step towards asserting yourself. Ultimately, this is good for you *and* good for them.

Nina's story

Nina loved her work but had a difficult relationship with her colleague Sarah. Despite her best efforts, Sarah hardly ever made eye contact and seemed to be constantly huffing or barking orders. Nina ended up feeling really anxious and worried and started to lose her confidence at work.

Is there a social situation or relationship you want to work on? If the answer is yes, jot it down and focus on why working on this is important to you. As you can see from Nina's example, she loved her job and working on her relationship with Sarah could potentially improve how she felt in and out of work.

_____

_____

_____

Step 2 Considering your own perspective with kindness

Think back to a specific situation that illustrates the difficulty you've had in a social situation and/or in a relationship with someone. Be as focused as you can. In Nina's case, she focused on the previous week, when she had tentatively said 'Hi' to Sarah, only to find she just carried on with her work. Make a note of the situation you want to focus on:

_____

_____

_____

 Building on the skills you have learnt in *The Kindness Workbook* so far, think back to the specific situation you've identified and have a go at the following exercise.

Extending your inner kindness towards yourself

1. Find somewhere to sit, free from distractions. When you're ready, sit in an upright yet relaxed position with your feet on the floor. Close your eyes or choose a focal point to look at, such as the base of a picture frame or mark on the floor.

2. Engage with your Soothing Rhythm Breathing (refer back to Chapter 8, page 146 if you need a recap), allowing your breathing to slow down. Focus your attention on your breath and just notice the flow of breathing in and breathing out.

3. Connect with your own inner kindness: the kindness you extend to others. Use your upright body posture and friendly facial expression to assist you. This might mean relaxing your shoulders, opening your chest and bringing a slight smile to your face. Spend time familiarising yourself with this important part of you.

4. When ready, from this perspective, imagine you're watching yourself in the specific situation you've decided to focus on. See the situation as though you're carefully watching a video playback.

When you're ready, gently bring the exercise to a close and widen your awareness to the chair that's supporting you and the room that you're in. If your eyes have been closed, open them; lift your gaze. Take some calming breaths and maybe have a stretch. Remaining connected with your inner kindness, answer the questions in the worksheet on the next page. Nina's answers might help guide you.

Inner Kindness Plan

Questions	Nina's answers	My answers
Why was this specific situation tricky?	I found the situation upsetting because I love my job and it's uncomfortable to be ignored It's important for me to get on with people	
If someone you cared about was in the same situation, what would you say to them?	I'm sorry you're going through all of this, it's going to be ok Of course this is upsetting	
Is there anything you could say to yourself that'd be helpful?	Maybe it's time to try another tactic to improve the situation	

Step 3 Considering other people's perspectives

Now let's consider the other person's (or people's) perspectives. Nina's examples and the Top Tips box below may help.

REFLECT

What might be going on for the other person and/or people? Could they be finding life tricky themselves? Do they know how you're feeling? Is there anything else that would be helpful to consider? For example, would it help to remind yourself that we're all the product of our biology and experiences and that we're all more similar than different – we're all just trying to get by?

Taking time to consider Sarah's perspective Nina calmly wrote:

I don't see Sarah interacting with anyone... so maybe it can't be that personal. She could be preoccupied by something, find interactions hard or maybe I've upset her in some way I'm not aware of. She doesn't seem the kind of person to get angry or argue so maybe she will be able to have a conversation with me - if I try to start one.

- It can be difficult to consider situations from another person's perspective. This might be because we feel hurt or simply find it difficult to consider what's going on for them. If this is the case, consider getting another 'mind' involved. Is there someone whose opinion you value and trust?

Step 4 Creating an assertive formula

Assertiveness involves taking action rather than avoiding, retaliating or getting into an argument. It increases the likelihood of a positive outcome by boosting the chance you'll be taken seriously. There are two loose 'assertiveness formulas' below that can be helpful, but it's OK if you want to adapt them for the situation you're going to focus your efforts on.

- We use the word 'loose' because the formulas provided are suggestions and not meant to be followed to the letter. It's not like a chemistry lab, where slight deviations from the instructions could end up in an explosion, so experiment away!

Formula 1

I think/feel/need _____

This is because _____

I think it would be helpful if _____

Can we discuss this?

If Nina was to use this formula, it might look like this:

> I feel like we don't get on because we hardly ever speak. I think it'd be helpful if we get to know each other better. Can we discuss this?

Formula 2

When you do/say _____

I feel _____

I would prefer _____

Can we have a chat about it?

If Nina used this formula, it might look like this:

> When you don't speak to me I feel I've done something to upset you. I'd prefer it if we could talk more. Can we chat about it?

Examples of assertiveness formulas from other scenarios

'*I feel like* I'm not being taken seriously at work *because* none of the ideas I come up with are ever acted upon. *It'd help me* to have some feedback about the ideas I have so I can understand why they may not be viable. *Can we discuss this?*'

'*When you say* negative things about what I'm wearing *I feel* really rubbish and often go out of the house in a bad mood. I don't want to go out with my top on inside out, or knickers hanging out of my jeans, but if it's a matter of taste *I'd prefer it* if you didn't say anything or wait to be asked. *Can we talk about it?*'

'*I think* this torch isn't working properly because the battery is dead after only about 15 minutes. *I wonder if you can* have a look at it and either exchange it or fix it?'

Now it's over to you. After playing around with some ideas, write down your own assertive statement below. Remember it's a statement that helps you express yourself while also holding the other person/people in mind.

_____

_____

_____

When you say, '*I feel ...*', '*I think ...*' or '*I need ...*' it leaves *less* opportunity for people to disagree with you. This is in stark contrast to saying, '*You make me ...*', '*You're out of order*' or '*You're winding me up*', which are more likely to trigger disagreement. As such, these assertive ways of expressing ourselves are often called 'I' statements, in contrast to 'You' statements.

Step 5 Hatching a Pre, During and After Plan (PDA Plan)

Before you take action, there are a number of additional ideas to take into account. Here are a few of them. Maybe you can think of more and add them to your PDA Plan.

Timing!

Despite what some people say, timing isn't everything. However, it can have a big bearing on how things go. For example, Nina might have carefully planned how to start a conversation with Sarah but if she's busy it's not likely to have the desired effect! So, consider when the best time to start the conversation would be.

Voice tone

As discovered throughout the book, tone of voice has a *HUGE* impact on how words are received. So, consider what tone of voice to use during your assertive conversation.

Body posture, movement and facial expression

Experiment with your body posture, movement and facial expression prior to taking action. For example, would it be less threatening for you to speak with someone face-to-face or maybe while you're both side-by-side engaging in an activity? Could tension in your face, although reasonable, make it more likely for the other person to think you're being confrontational?

Think back to the example of people talking in the cinema. How might your body posture and facial expression help you there?

Practise, practise, practise, practise, practise, practise, practise, practise, practise, practise, practise

Unfortunately, practice rarely makes perfect but it can definitely help. Have a look at some Top Tips that will help you prepare for action.

TOP TIPS

- Practise saying what you're hoping to say out loud (when you're on your own) and then while you're looking in the mirror. Adjust your body posture, facial expression and voice tone until it feels right.

- Make an audio or video recording of what you're planning on saying and – importantly – *HOW* you're planning on saying it, and review it.

- Get other people who have your best interests at heart involved and ask for constructive feedback on what you're saying and how you're saying it.

- Role-play the situation with someone you trust. Ask the other person to say very little at the start and later ask them to be a little more difficult. Another person's support and feedback may be incredibly helpful.

- Consider ideas and practices from other chapters of *The Kindness Workbook*. How about using your Kindness Crusader, Cheerleader, Coach, Supportive Friend, Superhero and/or Compassionate Companion (Chapter 6), affirmations (Chapter 13), and/or ladder of goals (Chapter 12)?

Creating a Pre, During and After Plan

You may remember generating a PDA Plan in Chapter 13. It involves creating a strategy to follow before, during and after events. Have a look at Nina's Plan and then complete your own on the worksheet provided.

Nina's Pre, During and After Plan

The Challenge : Resolving the difficulty with Sarah		
Pre	During	After
I've created an assertive statement using one of the formulas, considered my tone of voice and body posture so I'll practise this 'as and when' I'll wear my favourite comfy jumper and make sure I have lavender oil to help calm down I'll use my calm, peaceful place imagery exercise to help me prepare for the situation I'll arrange to see a friend afterwards so I can either celebrate or commiserate I'll try and get a good night's sleep and have breakfast that morning, so my body is in a good place I'll wear my 'your real strength comes from being your best you' badge I'll remind myself of Sarah's potential perspective on the situation and think about the potential benefits for both of us	I'll use my Soothing Rhythm Breathing I'll touch my soothing pebble in my pocket I'll remind myself that I'm living life in accordance with my values I'll be my own inner cheerleader	I'll use the Progressive Muscle Relaxation exercise to calm my body and mind I'll be kind to myself and remind myself, no matter how it's gone, it's a step in the right direction I'll remind myself I'm learning to be more assertive and that it takes courage to work on relationships and tackle difficult situations I'll write some notes on how it went

My Pre, During and After Plan

The Challenge:		
Pre	During	After

Once you have created the plan, your next step is to take action before reviewing your progress.

Step 6 Reviewing progress and considering further ways forward

Regardless of how things went, it's important to recognise the radical act you have just engaged in. It takes courage to work on tricky social situations and relationships in an assertive way, so give yourself a pat on the back for your good intentions and for having a go.

What did you learn from the situation? If it wasn't the outcome you had hoped for, jot down why this might have been the case.

REFLECT

_____

_____

_____

Nina wrote:

> So... That didn't go as expected. When I spoke with Sorah, she looked shocked to hear I was struggling with things. She's not happy in her job... So my job works for me, as a rung on the ladder for my career, whereas it doesn't work for her. I'm so glad I plucked up the courage to speak to her.
> It doesn't mean it's ok for her to be rude but I think it wasn't intentional on her part. I really do feel a lot better for raising it with her. I think it was a positive thing for Sorah too, my plucking up the courage to say something.

Are there any other situations or relationships that you can apply this skill to? You know the steps. It's now about climbing the next mountain – and when you get to the top, benefiting from all your hard work and effort.

- You can't plan for all situations (the cinema scenario at the start of this chapter is a great illustration of this); you may be put on the spot and need to say something quickly. In such situations pause and take a soothing breath, be mindful of your voice tone and body posture and remind yourself to be kind to yourself. The more you assert yourself, in a proactive or reactive way, the more natural it will become.

- Unfortunately, despite our best efforts, sometimes things don't improve and may even seem worse. This can be upsetting and frustrating. Give yourself a pat on the back for living life in accordance with your values and be kind to yourself going forward. If you're lucky to have the support of others, use it and consider what steps to take next.

My Kindness Box

Consider adding some of the written materials you have generated here to your Kindness Box. How about adding some affirmations that reflect the progress you've made, your PDA Plan, the formula that you decided to use or a sticky note congratulating yourself for the steps you have taken. Nina added a selfie of her and Sarah that reminded her of the positive changes she'd made for both of them. Cultivating assertive behaviour can have a powerful effect on your own and other people's lives. Having worked through the steps involved in asserting yourself, we hope you'll agree with the summary points below.

Summary

In this chapter, you have:

❖ Considered what assertiveness is

❖ Focused on your right to express how you feel

❖ Considered your own and other people's perspectives

❖ Used assertiveness formulas to resolve difficulties

❖ Created a PDA Plan

❖ Considered additions to your Kindness Box

Additional notes

What will help me be kinder to myself?

What can I add to my Kindness Box?

Finale: Moving forward

WELL DONE for getting to this point in your journey!

Having worked your way through the workbook, we hope you now know more about your wellbeing and how to improve it. We also hope your efforts have resulted in you initiating and experiencing some helpful, life-affirming changes. Of course, there may have been parts that you skim-read because the content was already familiar to you. There may also have been sections you avoided because you weren't ready (preferring to do the washing up instead!) that you might come back to in the future.

Wherever you're at in terms of this journey it's helpful to take stock and recognise the changes you've made and sketch a path for your future. This is what the finale is all about. Molly and Josh will come along with us for the ride!

Moving forward

Life can be amazing but (as we're sure you know) can be tricky too, so it's important to take stock regularly and acknowledge your *progress* and *achievements*, big AND small, because this creates a great platform from which you can grow. Going forward, it's helpful to remind ourselves of the knowledge and skills we've learnt that will help us navigate future ups and downs. Because time travels forwards and not backwards (unless you have a Tardis!), it's a great idea to set goals, creating a direction of travel for the future. So, for the final time, let's take a look at the chapter plan.

In this finale, you're going to:

- Look at your progress and achievements
- Create a short-term and long-term plan for the 'Future You'
- Consider a variety of activities to try in the future
- Create an inspirational vision board
- Think about what to add to your Kindness Box

We began *The Kindness Workbook* recognising that life can be difficult. There's so much to juggle and sometimes a little help is required. With this in mind, we've shared information, ideas and practices to help you overcome obstacles and boost your wellbeing.

Part 1 made the case for kindness, and we shared our K.I.N.D.N.E.S.S. mnemonic (helping you see what you're already doing and generating new ideas to try). You focused on understanding yourself (and others) and identified your values. *Part 2* explored attention, mindfulness and imagery, shared building blocks for everyday life, foundation skills and practices. In *Part 3* you focused on 'the fabulous four' of physiology, feelings, thoughts and behaviour. In this finale we start by celebrating your progress and achievements.

Appreciating and acknowledging achievements

We often fail to allow our achievements to 'sink in'. We're too quick to simply focus on the next goal or challenge. So before you start to consider your onward journey, take a few moments to allow your progress and achievements to sink in. Taking time to reflect and acknowledge your accomplishments (no matter how big or small) can give your wellbeing a boost. If you need a reminder, flick through the entries you've made in this book.

Let's have a look at Molly's story, the changes she's made and what she's learnt and achieved as she's worked her way through *The Kindness Workbook*. You'll find there's space for you to write about the changes you've made and what you've learnt and achieved.

Molly had noticed she'd started becoming self-conscious and had recently avoided going out with her friends. Molly bought The Kindness Workbook *because she wanted to feel more confident in social situations.*

Molly's Achievements

Kindness Certificate

Changes I've made and strategies that have helped me	• I've said yes to going out with friends more than I've done in the past • I've tried to speak up more in meetings and although I don't feel 100 per cent comfortable yet, it's a work in progress • Creating a vision board was useful because it's a visual reminder of what I want to achieve • The PDA plan helped me face my fear of social situations
What I've learnt and achieved	• I've learnt that avoiding situations doesn't help me in the long run • I've learnt that I can be a bit too critical of myself at times • I've got to the end of the book so that's an achievement • I'm more mindful, which means I'm spending less time worrying about the future and the past

My Achievements

Kindness Certificate

Changes I've made and strategies that have helped me

What I've learnt and achieved

Research has shown that when people look in the mirror and speak to themselves the way they would speak to a good friend, they experience a boost in mood and a reduction in self-criticism.

Once you have written your list of achievements, read them out loud to yourself, in the mirror. Allow what you've written to sink in. If you find it difficult, imagine you're speaking to someone you really care about.

REFLECT

What did you notice?

_____

_____

_____

Molly wrote:

> That was really tricky at first...it's hard looking at yourself in the mirror saying nice, kind things to yourself. It got easier after a bit and I did feel quite proud.

Deciding on a direction of travel

Having acknowledged your progress and achievements, let's now turn our attention to the 'Future You'. Remember the K.I.N.D.N.E.S.S. mnemonic that we looked at in Chapter 1? The mnemonic focused on the eight key kindness ingredients that build, boost and maintain wellbeing. You might find it helpful to revisit the chart you completed (pages 24–5) and reflect on the answers you gave at the time.

Let's now spend some time thinking about the future you. Moving forward, what would you like to continue to do, introduce or learn that will boost your wellbeing?

The 'Future You'

Holding in mind the K.I.N.D.N.E.S.S. mnemonic, consider what you want to achieve or try out in your short- and long-term future.

- Your goals can range from opening up or asserting yourself with other people right through to spending time on your own. They may involve getting up close and personal with a spider, going along to a new group or visiting your GP to talk about something that's bothering you. Some of your goals may involve self-care or doing something new, while others may focus on maintaining or re-engaging in certain activities.

- You might have generated one challenge or goal or a zillion. If you've got one big goal remember to break it down into smaller, more achievable goals – and don't forget to start with the easiest challenge first!

Have a look at Josh's story, his plan for his 'Future Self' and the list of potentially fun, educational and pleasurable activities you may wish to try. You'll see that the space is divided into things you would like to do in both the short and long term.

As you develop your plan, kindness is key, so think about how you can be kind to yourself as you plan to move forward.

Josh appreciated the changes he'd made to his well-being and was committed to both maintain and make additional improvements in the future. Josh had created vision boards, mind maps, reflected on his values, created playlists and used photography to help him express his feelings. Josh felt that creating a 'Future Self' Plan would be a good way to continue to boost his wellbeing.

Josh's Plan for His Future Self

My future Self		
My plans for the future	Short term (over the next few weeks and months)	Long term (over 12 months and longer)
Education and/or Work	Continue to spend time revising for next month's exams Submit my application for university Prepare to move away to university	Find a part-time job while I'm at university Check out what social activities and sports teams the university have that I may be interested in
Family and social life	Have quality time with my family and friends before I go to university	Keep in touch with my family and friends while I'm at university Invite my brother Jake over to stay with me
Things on my 'Bucket List' I need to prepare for	Save up money so I can go to Ibiza next year with Jake, Lily and Faye	Go to Ibiza
Personal e.g. activities I'd like to try that I may find fun and pleasurable	Talk more to other people Practise mindfulness I'd like to have a go at baking My mate Frankie loves baking so I'll have a chat with him and get some pointers - sounds like it could be fun	Improve confidence Be more mindful Find a new hobby that I like
Other e.g. health, fitness and self-care	Prepare for a 10km run by improving my health and fitness gradually	Raise money for charity by doing a 10km run

My Plan for My Future Self

My future Self		
My plans for the future	Short term (over the next few weeks and months)	Long term (over 12 months and longer)
Education and/ or Work		
Family and Social life		
Things on My 'Bucket List' I need to prepare for		
Personal e.g. activities I'd like to try that I May find fun and pleasurable		
Other e.g. health, fitness and self-care		

'Joy is not found in finishing an activity but in doing it.'
– Greg Anderson

Activities you may find fun, educational and/or pleasurable

If you're struggling for ideas, have a look at the list of activities that boost wellbeing. Maybe highlight with different coloured pens the activities that you would like to have a go at over the next few weeks and months. Some people like to share their list with friends and family and work through some of the activities together.

Activities that can boost wellbeing

Creative

- Drawing or painting
- Cooking and baking
- Writing – poems, lyrics or a diary
- Singing
- Playing an instrument
- Creating posts for social media
- Having a hobby
- Doing arts and crafts
- Photography
- Acting
- Dancing
- Making pottery
- Making a gift for someone
- Making something for yourself

Social/Entertaining/Fun

- Going out with a friend
- Visiting family or friends
- Going to or arranging a party
- Giving someone a compliment or saying well done to someone
- Chatting to someone at the bus stop
- Inviting a friend round to your house
- Going to the cinema
- Going to a sports event
- Playing a game
- Meeting new people
- Trying a new skill e.g. skating
- Flying a kite
- Going to a pleasure park

Self-care

- Buying something new for yourself
- Relaxing
- Exercising
- Buying your favourite food
- Visiting a health club – spa day
- Having your hair cut
- Watching your favourite TV programme
- Getting a good night's sleep
- Having a massage
- Buying yourself some flowers
- Going for a walk
- Planning a holiday
- Going to the beach
- Acknowledging accomplishments
- Meditating
- Playing with animals
- Being pampered – getting a pedicure or manicure

Educational

- Reading a book
- Enrolling on a course
- Doing a crossword or puzzle
- Learning to play a musical instrument
- Visiting a museum
- Making plans for the future
- Having a debate with friends
- Visiting an art gallery or theatre
- Visiting a zoo or animal sanctuary
- Learning something new
- Following a nature trail

Vision board

You may also like to create a vision board (or update the boards you created in previous chapters) focusing on the 'Future You'. Making a vision board is a creative way of helping you visualise your future. Once again, you could draw, paint, or cut out pictures from magazines, which inspire you to think about the things you want to strive for in the future. For example, on Josh's vision board he included a picture that reminded him that he wanted to go to university.

- It might be helpful to consider taking a photo of your vision board so that you have a picture of it on your phone.

We've now come to the end of our journey together. We would like to say well done for working through the ideas and practices in *The Kindness Workbook* and we wish you well for the future. But before you go (and for one last time) consider what you could add to your Kindness Box.

My Kindness Box

Josh added his 'Future Self' Plan, whereas Molly added a note *'If I do start to avoid situations again then I'll be sure to speak to my friends because they always encourage me . . . and maybe I can do that for myself too.'*

Throughout your journey, you've created and added to your Kindness Box. It's worth spending time reminding yourself of what you have in there. Perhaps there's nothing left to add – it might be overflowing! We've included an image of an empty box because you might find it helpful to write a list of what you have in your Kindness Box here. Alternatively, you may prefer to write something that inspires you on the image of the box.

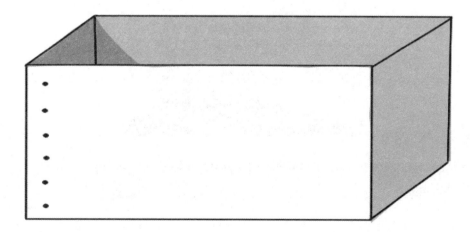

Summary

You have:

❖ Looked back at what you have learnt and achieved

❖ Created a short-term and long-term plan for the 'Future You'

❖ Made a vision board to help you focus on some of the things you want in your future

❖ Considered additions to your Kindness Box

Additional notes:

As you go forward, please use KINDNESS as your guide, sprinkling it into your life and sharing it with others.

Resource bank

In this section you will find additional worksheets and a list of websites where you will find further information about some of the approaches that have influenced this book. There's also a list of charities that provide support for young people.

Acceptance and Commitment Therapy (ACT)
Association for Contextual and Behavioural Science
https://contextualscience.org/act

Cognitive Behavioural Therapy (CBT)
British Association of Behavioural and Cognitive Psychotherapies
https://cbtregisteruk.com/About-BABCP.aspx

Compassion Focused Therapy (CFT)
Compassionate Mind Foundation
https://www.compassionatemind.co.uk/

Counselling
British Association for Counselling and Psychotherapy
https://www.bacp.co.uk/

Helpful websites
Anxiety UK https://www.anxietyuk.org.uk/
Heads Together https://www.headstogether.org.uk/
Place2Be https://www.place2be.org.uk/
Prince's Trust https://www.princes-trust.org.uk/
Rainbow Mind https://rainbowmind.org/
Samaritans https://www.samaritans.org/
YoungMinds https://youngminds.org.uk/

My Coping Strategies Worksheet

My worry, fear or concern	Situation that last triggered a worry, fear or concern	Coping Strategy Before	Coping Strategy During	Coping Strategy After

My Benefits and Drawbacks Worksheet

Benefits of my coping Strategies	Drawbacks of my coping Strategies

Understanding Myself Worksheet

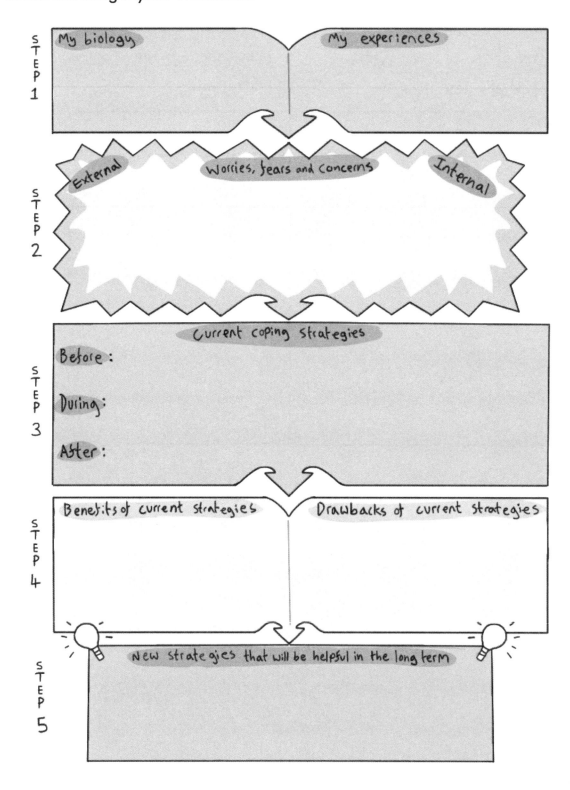

My Tree of Life

My Nourishment Worksheet

Nourishment	Things I used to do and want to continue	New ideas/things to try
Eating		
Drinking		
Personal benefits I'm likely to achieve		

My Activity Plan

Activities to reintroduce	Activities to try
Personal benefits I'm likely to achieve	

My Sleep Plan

Things that have helped me get a good night's sleep in the past	Exercises from The Kindness Workbook that could help	New ideas to try

Personal benefits I'm likely to achieve

Boosting My Wellbeing Worksheet

Additional ideas to give my wellbeing a boost
Personal benefits I'm likely to achieve

My Version of Me Worksheet

The version of me I'm cultivating and strengthening: _____ Body posture and movements: _____ Facial expression: _____ Breathing: _____	
Practise	How did it go?

My Feelings Worksheet

My Feelings Worksheet

Anger Fear Anxiety Disgust Joy Pride Relaxed Sadness Shame Guilt Happiness

Feeling	What triggered the feeling? Who was I with?	How did my body respond? Did I notice physical sensations in my stomach, head, neck, heart and/or face?	How did I react? What did I do/want to do? Did I want to run away, hide, hit out, cry, jump for joy or phone someone?			

My situation

Three Good Things Worksheet

Day of the week	1st good thing	2nd good thing	3rd good thing
Sunday			
Monday			
Tuesday			
Wednesday			
Thursday			
Friday			
Saturday			

My Mind Map

My Thoughts and Me Worksheet

Time of day	What thought went through your mind? Did you notice any mental images?	What physical reactions did you notice? Palpitations, sweaty palms, dry mouth, dizziness	What feelings were associated with the thought/image?	What did you do? Were there any behaviours associated with the thought? Did you try and avoid the thought or react to it?
Morning				
Afternoon				
Evening				

My Thought Balancing Worksheet

Thought	Evidence for my thoughts	Evidence against my thoughts	A balanced view

My Pros and Cons of Change Worksheet

Pros	Cons
What will be the benefits of _____	What will be the drawbacks if I don't _____ _____

My Ladder of Goals

Remember to put the easiest goal at the bottom of the ladder and the most difficult at the top.

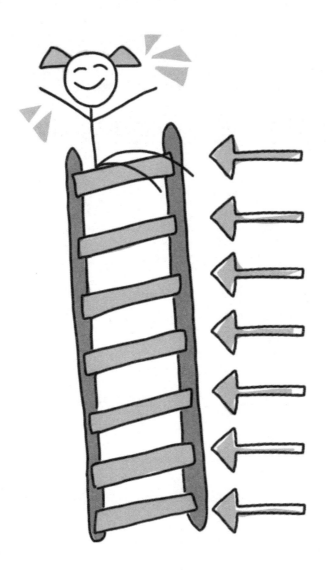

My Pre, During and After Plan

The challenge:		
Pre the challenge	During the challenge	After the challenge

My Plan for My Future Self

My future Self		
My plans for the future	Short term (over the next few weeks and months)	Long term (over 12 months and longer)
Education and/ or Work		
Family and Social life		
Things on My 'Bucket List' I need to prepare for		
Personal e.g. activities I'd like to try that I May find fun and pleasurable		
Other e.g. health, fitness and self-care		

Index

Note: page numbers in **bold** refer to Worksheets, page numbers in *italics* refer to diagrams.